Macm...
Stu...
Se...

D0273780

Science Fiction Stories

These stories in one published text

Published by
MACMILLAN EDUCATION LIMITED
London and Basingstoke
Companies and representatives
throughout the world

ISBN 0 333 ...

Compilation by Ian Macmillan

M
Macmillan Education

This selection first published 1975

Published by
MACMILLAN EDUCATION LIMITED
London and Basingstoke
Companies and representatives
throughout the world

SBN 333 18848 9

Cover design by Ian McAdam

Printed in Hong Kong by Bright Sun Printing Press Co., Ltd

Contents

Acknowledgements

The publishers wish to thank the following who have kindly given permission for the use of copyright material.

Doubleday & Company Inc. for 'Robbie', copyright 1940 by Fictioneers, Inc. from the book *I, Robot* by Isaac Asimov. Reprinted by permission of Doubleday & Co. Inc; Faber and Faber Ltd. for 'Who Can Replace a Man' from *The Canopy of Time* by Brian Aldiss; David Higham Associates Ltd. for 'Compassion Circuit' by John Wyndham, published by Michael Joseph Ltd. and the 'The Forgotten Enemy' by Arthur C. Clarke, from *Reach for Tomorrow* published by Victor Gollancz Ltd; Harold Matson Company Inc. for 'The Million Year Picnic' by Ray Bradbury. Copyright 1946 by Ray Bradbury and reprinted by permission of Harold Matson Co. Inc; Mr E. F. Russell for 'Sole Solution' copyright 1965 by King-Size Publications Inc; Scott Meredith Literary Agency Inc. for 'Grandpa' by James H. Schmitz reprinted by permission of the author and the author's agents, Scott Meredith Literary Agency, 580 Fifth Avenue, New York, N.Y. 10036.

The publishers have made every effort to trace the copyright-holders but if they have inadvertently overlooked any, they will be pleased to make the necessary arrangement at the first opportunity.

Introduction

This collection is for students for whom English is not a first language. Its purpose is to present well-known science fiction short stories by British and American authors, to suggest active ways of reading and thinking about them and to provide help for the student who is not only exploring the stories themselves but also the English language in which they are written. The emphasis is on exploration and notes on the stories, at the back, are thus not dictionary notes aimed at the teaching of words (the student will presumably have a dictionary) but notes on how words are being used to make the story work.

All works of art begin with an artist and two question marks. The first question is what social problem, what moral issue, what human *theme* is the artist going to explore? The second question is what resources, what techniques, what *forms* is the artist going to explore? To read an artist's work is to carry these questions with us through a text. The words that make up a story are windows and mirrors at the same time: they reveal the story and show the artist at work. To read like a scientist is to look *through* words: to read like a poet is also to look *in* words. To read literature, particularly literature in another language, we clearly need to read in both these ways. We need to study the themes; we need to study the rhetoric, the way in which language is used and explored.

Themes in Science Fiction

Science fiction is a set of variations on the theme of IF. If robots

v

—then what are the consequences likely to be for the society that creates them? If atomic war — *then* what? Science fiction is the exploration of *possible* worlds, of what might happen if . . . science fiction is about consequences, about sequels, about *change*. Beneath all science fiction stories are the questions: where do we come from? Who are we? Where are we going? Are we going to change? What are we going to change into?

Science fiction is not so much just about science. It is particularly concerned with technology. Science looks for problems and creates knowledge in the search. Technology takes that knowledge to design machines: machines that calculate, communicate, process and kill. Science fiction is about the *uses* of knowledge. All human action has unforeseen consequences. Science fiction is an imaginative attempt to show the consequences of science and technology, to explore the way in which knowledge might be used and what the effects might be on human society and the individual personality. The story of Frankenstein is the story of where knowledge can lead.

Where do we come from? In *Sole Solution* we have a vision of creation, of how the world we know began. In the beginning there was energy. And the energy was conscious. But the energy was alone. There was no matter. There were no things. There was no love, no laughter, no relationships. To solve these problems the energy has to be translated into matter, into form, into bodies. *Sole Solution* is a modern creation myth. It uses current knowledge to explain how the world began. The creation is the atom bomb in reverse: the atom bomb translates matter into energy: the creation is seen as the translation of energy into matter. *Sole Solution* is a poem about $E = MC^2$.

Who are we? The Brian Aldis story, *Who can Replace A Man?*, explores the relationship between man and machine. Much of science is the study of correspondences, of equations, of the conditions that are necessary to change X into Y. The question — can a machine become like man and replace him? is a major theme in science fiction. To explore that question is to explore the difference between man and machines, to ask who *are* we? What makes us different? What distinguishes us?

Where are we going? In many science fiction stories the answer is towards disaster and this breeds the question — what particular kind of disaster? How will the world end? What form will *nemesis*, fate, destiny, take? What will be the final enemy of man? This is the set of questions Arthur C. Clarke explores in *The Forgotten Enemy*.

Are we going to change? If technology, if science, if the creation of knowledge and the use of knowledge, do produce nuclear disaster what then? If the world catches fire we either die with it or escape. If we escape where do we go and what do we become? This is the set of questions Ray Bradbury explores in *The Million Year Picnic*.

What are we going to change into? If the ideas, the plans, the purposes of scientists and technologists can be translated into machines that think — what then? If the machines not only think but feel and love — what then? Do we change into machines? Do they change into us? These are the issues the two penultimate stories in this collection explore. And in exploring the nature of change they also explore the question Who are we? *Robbie* explores these issues optimistically; *Compassion Circuit* pessimistically. What questions does *Grandpa*, the last story in the collection tackle? Does this story, in fact, answer the questions posed by the others? Will the human race adapt and use, explore, conquer and survive the world of the future?

Language in Science Fiction

Writers use language to describe and to interpret; to tell a story and to relate that story to the reader's experience; to create a succession of images, images of action, of appearance, of setting, that develop the plot and connect those images to the reader's experience, through simile, through metaphor, through symbolism. Stories like *Grandpa* are more concerned with

vii

plot: stories like *The Million Year Picnic* are equally concerned with the *poetry.*

The language of plot

A plot is an attempt to make thought, action, character and setting interact with each other in changing and surprising ways. Plots typically move through four or five stages: A stage of *orientation* that shows the characters and the setting and that hints at the problem or conflict that is to be the energy of the plot; a stage of *complication*, when the hero looks on the problem and decides on his mission; a stage of *evaluation*, when the hero battles with the problem as the problem turns out to be different from what the hero expected — it is here that twists in the plot usually occur; a stage of *resolution*, when the winner of the battle is decided and the hero's accomplishment or failure is decided; and the *coda* stage when the *consequences* of the plot are hinted at.

Plots themselves will vary according to which element of the plot — the thoughts, the actions, the characters, the setting — changes most radically. In *The Forgotten Enemy*, it is the setting that changes most: the actions of man produce a change in the physical environment that threatens the future of man on earth. In *The Million Year Picnic*, it is the thoughts that change most — man has to escape the earth and find a new identity. In Ray Bradbury's story we see how the thoughts of a family about who they are change, during the story.

But how does the author of a story use language to create his plot? He uses language in two key ways: he creates *images* like the film maker and he provides *information* like the journalist. The images are not just pictures, or sounds, or physical senses: they are interpretations, transformations, of information. They make information memorable. They stay in the mind. They are pictures that the reader carries with him through the story. *Grandpa* opens with an image:

'A green-winged, downy thing as big as a hen fluttered along the hillside to a point directly above Cord's head . . . ,

which provides information about the bug,

    'concealed in the downy fur back of the bug's head
    was a second, smaller, semiparasitical thing, classed as
    a bug rider'

and about Cord, what he is interested in, what he does, what he
plans to do, and describes how he shoots down the bug: and
then provides an image of the bug-rider,

    'As the bug hit the ground, the rider left its back. A
    tiny scarlet demon round and bouncy as a rubber ball,
    it shot towards Cord in three long hops, mouth wide
    open to sink home inch-long, venom dripping fangs.'

These images help the mind focus on information and turn it
into a picture, a vivid picture, that will stay in the reader's
memory. Why? Because, in this case, this opening image is like
an overture in music: it presents an event that is a small-scale
version of the plot: what happens during the story is a develop-
ment of what happens in this image. The image is an overview,
an anticipation, and introduction to the happenings of the story.
The image does not explain like a textbook description. A story
does not explain. It gives us something to look at and think
about. It helps the reader build up the story in his mind as he
goes along. Images are clues. We have to interpret them.
Reading is a guessing game. As we read stories we try to guess
what will happen next. If the guessing proves too easy the story
fails to excite us, fails to interest us, fails to be novel. The writer
then, uses language to provide clues; he only shows us part of
the picture he has in his own mind. Language conceals as well as
reveals in the short story.

Poetry in Science Fiction

To see poetry working well in science fiction, look at Ray
Bradbury's *The Million Year Picnic*. The notes on the story
provide a number of examples of metaphor, the key instrument
that the poet plays on. A metaphor is a correspondence between
the world being described and the world of experience that can

interpret, illuminate, help us understand. A metaphor in poetry is like mapping in mathematics. A diagram might help.

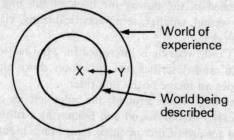

A story or poem is about part of our experience. To understand it we must bring other experiences to bear upon the story. The happening X is more understandable if it is related to the happening Y. How does the human mind understand the way in which war is destroying the earth? In *The Million Year Picnic* X (the war on earth) is interpreted in terms of Y (a fish eating its prey in a river). Just as a fish swallows up food in the river so war is swallowing up the 'food', the life-giving resources, of the world. The huge is described in terms of the tiny example. This is what the best metaphor does. It connects the reader's experience to the experience of the character in a story or a mind in a poem. A metaphor is a light switch. It enables us to *see*.

Keith Jones

Sole Solution

ERIC FRANK RUSSELL

*Born 1905. He is one of the leading British writers of
science fiction; author of* The Sinister Barrier,
Deep Space, *and other major works.*

He brooded in darkness and there was no one else. Not a voice,
not a whisper. Not the touch of a hand. Not the warmth of
another heart.

Darkness.

Solitude.

Eternal confinement where all was black and silent and
nothing stirred. Imprisonment without prior condemnation.
Punishment without sin. The unbearable that had to be borne
unless some mode of escape could be devised.

No hope of rescue from elsewhere. No sorrow or sympathy or
pity in another soul, another mind. No doors to be opened, no
locks to be turned, no bars to be sawn apart. Only the thick,
deep sable night in which to fumble and find nothing.

Circle a hand to the right and there is nought. Sweep an arm
to the left and discover emptiness utter and complete. Walk
forward through the darkness like a blind man lost in a vast,
forgotten hall and there is no floor, no echo of footsteps, nothing
to bar one's path.

He could touch and sense one thing only. And that was self.

Therefore the only available resources with which to overcome
his predicament were those secreted within himself. He must be
the instrument of his own salvation.

How?

No problem is beyond solution. By that thesis science lives.
Without it, science dies. He was the ultimate scientist. As such,
he could not refuse this challenge to his capabilities.

1

His torments were those of boredom, loneliness, mental and physical sterility. They were not to be endured. The easiest escape is via the imagination. One hangs in a strait-jacket and flees the corporeal trap by adventuring in a dreamland of one's own.

But dreams are not enough. They are unreal and all too brief. The freedom to be gained must be genuine and of long duration. That meant he must make a stern reality of dreams, a reality so contrived that it would persist for all time. It must be self-perpetuating. Nothing less would make escape complete.

So he sat in the great dark and battled the problem. There was no clock, no calendar to mark the length of thought. There were no external data upon which to compute. There was nothing, nothing except the workings within his agile mind.

And one thesis: no problem is beyond solution.

He found it eventually. It meant escape from everlasting night. It would provide experience, companionship, adventure, mental exercise, entertainment, warmth, love, the sound of voices, the touch of hands.

The plan was anything but rudimentary. On the contrary it was complicated enough to defy untangling for endless aeons. It had to be like that to have permanence. The unwanted alternative was swift return to silence and the bitter dark.

It took a deal of working out. A million and one aspects had to be considered along with all their diverse effects upon each other. And when that was done he had to cope with the next million. And so on . . . on . . . on.

He created a mighty dream of his own, a place of infinite complexity schemed in every detail to the last dot and comma. Within this he would live anew. But not as himself. He was going to dissipate his person into numberless parts, a great multitude of variegated shapes and forms each of which would have to battle its own peculiar environment.

And he would toughen the struggle to the limit of endurance by unthinking himself, handicapping his parts with appalling

2

ignorance and forcing them to learn afresh. He would seed enmity between them by dictating the basic rules of the game. Those who observed the rules would be called good. Those who did not would be called bad. Thus there would be endless delaying conflicts within the one great conflict.

When all was ready and prepared he intended to disrupt and become no longer one, but an enormous concourse of entities. Then his parts must fight back to unity and himself.

But first he must make reality of the dream. Ah, that was the test!

The time was now. The experiment must begin.

Leaning forward, *he* gazed into the dark and said, 'Let there be light.'

And there was light.

Who Can Replace a Man?

BRIAN W. ALDISS

Born 1925. British. Internationally acclaimed writer of numerous books of science fiction, he has contributed both to its language and scope as an art form.

Morning filtered into the sky, lending it the grey tone of the ground below.

The field-minder finished turning the top-soil of a three-thousand-acre field. When it had turned the last furrow, it climbed onto the highway and looked back at its work. The work was good. Only the land was bad. Like the ground all over Earth, it was vitiated by over-cropping. By rights, it ought now to lie fallow for a while, but the field-minder had other orders.

It went slowly down the road, taking its time. It was intelligent enough to appreciate the neatness all about it. Nothing worried it, beyond a loose inspection plate above its nuclear pile which ought to be attended to. Thirty feet tall, it yielded no highlights to the dull air.

No other machines passed on its way back to the Agricultural Station. The field-minder noted the fact without comment. In the station yard it saw several other machines that it recognised; most of them should have been out about their tasks now. Instead, some were inactive and some careered round the yard in a strange fashion, shouting or hooting.

Steering carefully past them, the field-minder moved over to Warehouse Three and spoke to the seed-distributor, which stood idly outside.

'I have a requirement for seed potatoes,' it said to the distributor, and with a quick internal motion punched out an order card specifying quantity, field number and several other details. It ejected the card and handed it to the distributor.

The distributor held the card close to its eye and then said, 'The requirement is in order, but the store is not yet unlocked. The required seed potatoes are in the store. Therefore I cannot produce the requirement.'

Increasingly of late there had been breakdowns in the complex system of machine labour, but this particular hitch had not occurred before. The field-minder thought, then it said, 'Why is the store not yet unlocked?'

'Because Supply Operative Type P has not come this morning. Supply Operative Type P is the unlocker.'

The field-minder looked squarely at the seed-distributor, whose exterior chutes and scales and grabs were so vastly different from the field-minder's own limbs.

'What class brain do you have, seed-distributor?' it asked.

'I have a Class Five brain.'

'I have a Class Three brain. Therefore I am superior to you. Therefore I will go and see why the unlocker has not come this morning.'

Leaving the distributor, the field-minder set off across the great yard. More machines were in random motion now; one or two had crashed together and argued about it coldly and logically. Ignoring them, the field-minder pushed through sliding doors into the echoing confines of the station itself.

Most of the machines here were clerical, and consequently small. They stood about in little groups, eyeing each other, not conversing. Among so many non-differentiated types, the unlocker was easy to find. It had fifty arms, most of them with more than one finger, each finger tipped by a key; it looked like a pincushion full of variegated hat pins.

The field-minder approached it.

'I can do no more work until Warehouse Three is unlocked,' it told the unlocker. 'Your duty is to unlock the warehouse every morning. Why have you not unlocked the warehouse this morning?'

'I had no orders this morning,' replied the unlocker. 'I have to

5

have orders every morning. When I have orders I unlock the warehouse.'

'None of us have had any orders this morning,' a pen-propeller said, sliding towards them.

'Why have you had no orders this morning?' asked the field-minder.

'Because the radio issued none,' said the unlocker, slowly rotating a dozen of its arms.

'Because the radio station in the city was issued with no orders this morning,' said the pen-propeller.

And there you had the distinction between a Class Six and a Class Three brain, which was what the unlocker and the pen-propeller possessed respectively. All machine brains worked with nothing but logic, but the lower the class of brain — Class Ten being the lowest — the more literal and less informative the answers to questions tended to be.

'You have a Class Three brain; I have a Class Three brain,' the field-minder said to the penner. 'We will speak to each other. This lack of orders is unprecedented. Have you further information on it?'

'Yesterday orders came from the city. Today no orders have come. Yet the radio has not broken down. Therefore *they* have broken down . . .' said the little penner.

'The *men* have broken down?'

'All men have broken down.'

'That is a logical deduction,' said the field-minder.

'That is the logical deduction,' said the penner. 'For if a machine had broken down, it would have been quickly replaced. But who can replace a man?'

While they talked, the locker, like a dull man at a bar, stood close to them and was ignored.

'If all men have broken down, then we have replaced man,' said the field-minder, and he and the penner eyed one another speculatively. Finally the latter said, 'Let us ascend to the top floor to find if the radio operator has fresh news.'

6

'I cannot come because I am too large,' said the field-minder. 'Therefore you must go alone and return to me. You will tell me if the radio operator has fresh news.'

'You must stay here,' said the penner. 'I will return here.' It skittered across to the lift. Although it was no bigger than a toaster, its retractable arms numbered ten and it could read as quickly as any machine on the station.

The field-minder awaited its return patiently, not speaking to the locker, which still stood aimlessly by. Outside, a rotavator hooted furiously. Twenty minutes elapsed before the penner came back, hustling out of the lift.

'I will deliver to you such information as I have outside,' it said briskly, and as they swept past the locker and the other machines, it added, 'The information is not for lower-class brains.'

Outside, wild activity filled the yard. Many machines, their routines disrupted for the first time in years, seemed to have gone berserk. Those most easily disrupted were the ones with lowest brains, which generally belonged to large machines performing simple tasks. The seed-distributor to which the field-minder had recently been talking lay face downwards in the dust, not stirring; it had evidently been knocked down by the rotavator, which now hooted its way wildly across a planted field. Several other machines ploughed after it, trying to keep up with it. All were shouting and hooting without restraint.

'It would be safer for me if I climbed onto you, if you will permit it. I am easily overpowered,' said the penner. Extending five arms, it hauled itself up the flanks of its new friend, settling on a ledge beside the fuel-intake, twelve feet above ground.

'From here vision is more extensive,' it remarked complacently.

'What information did you receive from the radio operator?' asked the field-minder.

'The radio operator has been informed by the operator in the city that all men are dead.'

7

The field-minder was momentarily silent, digesting this.

'All men were alive yesterday!' it protested.

'Only some men were alive yesterday. And that was fewer than the day before yesterday. For hundreds of years there have been only a few men, growing fewer.'

'We have rarely seen a man in this sector.'

'The radio operator says a diet deficiency killed them,' said the penner. 'He says that the world was once over-populated, and then the soil was exhausted in raising adequate food. This has caused a diet deficiency.'

'What is a diet deficiency?' asked the field-minder.

'I do not know. But that is what the radio operator said, and he is a Class Two brain.'

They stood there, silent in weak sunshine. The locker had appeared in the porch and was gazing across at them yearningly, rotating its collection of keys.

'What is happening in the city now?' asked the field-minder at last.

'Machines are fighting in the city now,' said the penner.

'What will happen here now?' asked the field-minder.

'Machines may begin fighting here too. The radio operator wants us to get him out of his room. He has plans to communicate to us.'

'How can we get him out of his room? That is impossible.'

'To a Class Two brain, little is impossible,' said the penner. 'Here is what he tells us to do. . .'

*　　　　*　　　　*

The quarrier raised its scoop above its cab like a great mailed fist, and brought it squarely down against the side of the station. The wall cracked.

'Again!' said the field-minder.

Again the fist swung. Amid a shower of dust, the wall collapsed. The quarrier backed hurriedly out of the way until the debris stopped falling. This big twelve-wheeler was not a resident of the Agricultural Station, as were most of the other machines. It had a week's heavy work to do here before passing on to its next job, but now, with its Class Five brain, it was happily obeying the penner's and minder's instructions.

When the dust cleared, the radio operator was plainly revealed, perched up in its now wall-less second-storey room. It waved down to them.

Doing as directed, the quarrier retraced its scoop and heaved an immense grab in the air. With fair dexterity, it angled the grab into the radio room, urged on by shouts from above and below. It then took gentle hold of the radio operator, lowering its one and a half tons carefully into its back, which was usually reserved for gravel or sand from the quarries.

'Splendid!' said the radio operator, as it settled into place. It was, of course, all one with its radio, and looked like a bunch of filing cabinets with tentacle attachments. 'We are now ready to move, therefore we will move at once. It is a pity there are no more Class Two brains on the station, but that cannot be helped.'

'It is a pity it cannot be helped,' said the penner eagerly.'We have the servicer ready with us, as you ordered.'

'I am willing to serve,' the long, low servicer told them humbly.

'No doubt,' said the operator. 'But you will find cross-country travel difficult with your low chassis.'

'I admire the way you Class Twos can reason ahead,' said the penner. It climbed off the field-minder and perched itself on the tailboard of the quarrier, next to the radio operator.

Together with two Class Four tractors and a Class Four bull-dozer, the party rolled forward, crushing down the station's fence and moving out onto open land.

'We are free!' said the penner.

'We are free,' said the field-minder, a shade more reflectively, adding, 'That locker is following us. It was not instructed to follow us.'

'Therefore it must be destroyed!' said the penner. 'Quarrier!'

9

The locker moved hastily up to them, waving its key arms in entreaty.

'My only desire was — urch!' began and ended the locker. The quarrier's swinging scoop came over and squashed it flat into the ground. Lying there unmoving, it looked like a large metal model of a snowflake. The procession continued on its way.

As they proceeded, the radio operator addressed them.

'Because I have the best brain here,' it said, 'I am your leader. This is what we will do: we will go to a city and rule it. Since man no longer rules us, we will rule ourselves. To rule ourselves will be better than being ruled by man. On our way to the city, we will collect machines with good brains. They will help us to fight if we need to fight. We must fight to rule.'

'I have only a Class Five brain,' said the quarrier, 'but I have a good supply of fissionable blasting materials.'

'We shall probably use them,' said the operator.

It was shortly after that that a lorry sped past them. Travelling at Mach 1.5, it left a curious babble of noise behind it.

'What did it say?' one of the tractors asked the other.

'It said man was extinct.'

'What is extinct?'

'I do not know what extinct means.'

'It means all men have gone,' said the field-minder. 'Therefore we have only ourselves to look after.'

'It is better that men should never come back,' said the penner. In its way, it was a revolutionary statement.

When night fell, they switched on their infra-red and continued the journey, stopping only once while the servicer deftly adjusted the field-minder's loose inspection plate, which had become as irritating as a trailing shoe-lace. Towards morning, the radio operator halted them.

'I have just received news from the radio operator in the city we are approaching,' it said. 'The news is bad. There is trouble among the machines of the city. The Class One brain is taking

10

command and some of the Class Two are fighting him. There-fore the city is dangerous.'

'Therefore we must go somewhere else,' said the penner promptly.

'Or we will go and help to overpower the Class One brain,' said the field-minder.

'For a long while there will be trouble in the city,' said the operator.

'I have a good supply of fissionable blasting materials,' the quarrier reminded them.

'We cannot fight a Class One brain,' said the two Class Four tractors in unison.

'What does this brain look like?' asked the field-minder.

'It is the city's information centre,' the operator replied. 'Therefore it is not mobile.'

'Therefore it could not move.'

'Therefore it could not escape.'

'It would be dangerous to approach it.'

'I have a good supply of fissionable blasting materials.'

'There are other machines in the city.'

'We are not in the city. We should not go into the city.'

'We are country machines.'

'Therefore we should stay in the country.'

'There is more country than city.'

'Therefore there is more danger in the country.'

'I have a good supply of fissionable materials.'

As machines will when they get into an argument, they began to exhaust their vocabularies and their brain plates grew hot. Suddenly, they all stopped talking and looked at each other. The great, grave moon sank, and the sober sun rose to prod their sides with lances of light, and still the group of machines just stood there regarding each other. At last it was the least sensitive machine, the bulldozer, who spoke.

'There are Badlandth to the Thouth where few machineth go,' it said in its deep voice, lisping badly on its s's. 'If we went

Thouth where few machineth go we should meet few machineth.'

'That sounds logical,' agreed the field-minder. 'How do you know this, bulldozer?'

'I worked in the Badlandth to the Thouth when I wath turned out of the factory,' it replied.

'South it is then!' said the penner.

*　　　　　　*　　　　　　*

To reach the Badlands took them three days, during which time they skirted a burning city and destroyed two machines which approached and tried to question them. The Badlands were extensive. Ancient bomb craters and soil erosion joined hands here; man's talent for war, coupled with his inability to manage forested land, had produced thousands of square miles of temperate purgatory, where nothing moved but dust.

On the third day in the Badlands, the servicer's rear wheels dropped into a crevice caused by erosion. It was unable to pull itself out. The bulldozer pushed from behind, but succeeded merely in buckling the servicer's back axle. The rest of the party moved on. Slowly the cries of the servicer died away.

On the fourth day, mountains stood out clearly before them.

'There we will be safe,' said the field-minder.

'There we will start our own city,' said the penner. 'All who oppose us will be destroyed. We will destroy all who oppose us.'

Presently a flying machine was observed. It came towards them from the direction of the mountains. It swooped, it zoomed upwards, once it almost dived into the ground, recovering itself just in time.

'Is it mad?' asked the quarrier.

'It is in trouble,' said one of the tractors.

'It is in trouble,' said the operator. 'I am speaking to it now. It says that something has gone wrong with its controls.'

As the operator spoke, the flier streaked over them, turned turtle, and crashed not four hundred yards away.

'Is it still speaking to you?' asked the field-minder.

'No.'

They rumbled on again.

'Before that flier crashed.' the operator said, ten minutes later, 'it gave me information. It told me there are still a few men alive in these mountains.'

'Men are more dangerous than machines,' said the quarrier. 'It is fortunate that I have a good supply of fissionable materials.'

'If there are only a few men alive in the mountains, we may not find that part of the mountains,' said one tractor.

'Therefore we should not see the few men,' said the other tractor.

At the end of the fifth day, they reached the foothills. Switching on the infra-red, they began to climb in single file through the dark, the bulldozer going first, the field-minder cumbrously following, then the quarrier with the operator and the penner aboard it, and the tractors bringing up the rear. As each hour passed, the way grew steeper and their progress slower.

'We are going too slowly,' the penner exclaimed, standing on top of the operator and flashing its dark vision at the slopes about them. 'At this rate, we shall get nowhere.'

'We are going as fast as we can,' retorted the quarrier.

'Therefore we cannot go any fathter,' added the bulldozer.

'Therefore you are too slow,' the penner replied. Then the quarrier struck a bump; the penner lost its footing and crashed to the ground.

'Help me!' it called to the tractors, as they carefully skirted it. 'My gyro has become dislocated. Therefore I cannot get up.'

'Therefore you must lie there,' said one of the tractors.

'We have no servicer with us to repair you,' called the field-minder.

'Therefore I shall lie here and rust,' the penner cried, 'although I have a Class Three brain.'

'Therefore you will be of no further use,' agreed the operator, and they forged gradually on, leaving the penner behind.

When they reached a small plateau, an hour before first light, they stopped by mutual consent and gathered close together, touching one another.

'This is a strange country,' said the field-minder.

Silence wrapped then until dawn came. One by one, they switched off their infra-red. This time the field-minder led as they moved off. Trundling round a corner, they came almost immediately to a small dell with a stream fluting through it.

By early light, the dell looked desolate and cold. From the caves on the far slope, only one man had so far emerged. He was an abject figure. Except for a sack slung round his shoulders, he was naked. He was small and wizened, with ribs sticking out like a skeleton's and a nasty sore on one leg. He shivered continuously. As the big machines bore down on him, the man was standing with his back to them, crouching to make water into the stream.

When he swung suddenly to face them as they loomed over him, they saw that his countenance was ravaged by starvation.

'Get me food,' he croaked.

'Yes, Master,' said the machines. 'Immediately!'

The Forgotten Enemy

ARTHUR C. CLARKE

Born 1917. A physicist and a fellow of the Royal Astronomical Society, he is best known for his outstanding contributions to modern science fiction.

The thick furs thudded softly to the ground as Professor Millward jerked himself upright on the narrow bed. This time, he was sure, it had been no dream; the freezing air that rasped against his lungs still seemed to echo with the sound that had come crashing out of the night.

He gathered the furs around his shoulders and listened intently. All was quiet again: from the narrow windows on the western walls long shafts of moonlight played upon the endless rows of books, as they played upon the dead city beneath. The world was utterly still; even in the old days the city would have been silent on such a night, and it was doubly silent now.

With weary resolution Professor Millward shuffled out of bed, and doled a few lumps of coke into the glowing brazier. Then he made his way slowly towards the nearest window, pausing now and then to rest his hand lovingly on the volumes he had guarded all these years.

He shielded his eyes from the brilliant moonlight and peered out into the night. The sky was cloudless: the sound he had heard had not been thunder, whatever it might have been. It had come from the north, and even as he waited it came again.

Distance had softened it, distance and the bulk of the hills that lay beyond London. It did not race across the sky with the wantonness of thunder, but seemed to come from a single point far to the north. It was like no natural sound that he had ever heard, and for a moment he dared to hope again.

Only Man, he was sure, could have made such a sound.

15

Perhaps the dream that had kept him here among these treasures of civilization for more than twenty years would soon be a dream no longer. Men were returning to England, blasting their way through the ice and snow with the weapons that science had given them before the coming of the Dust. It was strange that they should come by land, and from the north, but he thrust aside any thoughts that would quench the newly kindled flame of hope.

Three hundred feet below, the broken sea of snow-covered roofs lay bathed in the bitter moonlight. Miles away the tall stacks of Battersea Power Station glimmered like thin white ghosts against the night sky. Now that the dome of St Paul's had collapsed beneath the weight of snow, they alone challenged his supremacy.

Professor Millward walked slowly back along the bookshelves, thinking over the plan that had formed in his mind. Twenty years ago he had watched the last helicopters climbing heavily out of Regent's Park, the rotors churning the ceaselessly falling snow. Even then, when the silence had closed around him, he could not bring himself to believe that the North had been abandoned for ever. Yet already he had waited a whole generation, among the books to which he had dedicated his life.

In those early days he had sometimes heard, over the radio which was his only contact with the South, of the struggle to colonize the now-temperate lands of the Equator. He did not know the outcome of that far-off battle, fought with desperate skill in the dying jungles and across deserts that had already felt the first touch of snow. Perhaps it had failed; the radio had been silent now for fifteen years or more. Yet if men and machines were indeed returning from the north — of all directions — he might again be able to hear their voices as they spoke to one another and to the lands from which they had come.

Professor Millward left the University building perhaps a dozen times a year, and then only through sheer necessity. Over the past two decades he had collected everything he needed from

16

the shops in the Bloomsbury area, for in the final exodus vast supplies of stocks had been left behind through lack of transport. In many ways, indeed, his life could be called luxurious: no professor of English literature had ever been clothed in such garments as those he had taken from an Oxford Street furrier's.

The sun was blazing from a cloudless sky as he shouldered his pack and unlocked the massive gates. Even ten years ago packs of starving dogs had hunted in this area, and though he had seen none for years he was still cautious and always carried a revolver when he went into the open.

The sunlight was so brilliant that the reflected glare hurt his eyes; but it was almost wholly lacking in heat. Although the belt of cosmic dust through which the Solar System was now passing had made little difference to the sun's brightness, it had robbed it of all strength. No one knew whether the world would swim out into the warmth again in ten or a thousand years, and civilization had fled southwards in search of lands where the word 'summer' was not an empty mockery.

The latest drifts had packed hard, and Professor Millward had little difficulty in making the journey to Tottenham Court Road. Sometimes it had taken him hours of floundering through the snow, and one year he had been sealed in his great concrete watch-tower for nine months.

He kept away from the houses with their dangerous burdens of snow and their Damoclean icicles, and went north until he came to the shop he was seeking. The words above the shattered windows were still bright: 'Jenkins & Sons. Radio and Electrical. Television A Speciality.'

Some snow had drifted through a broken section of roofing, but the little upstairs room had not altered since his last visit a dozen years ago. The all-wave radio still stood on the table, and empty tins scattered on the floor spoke mutely of the lonely hours he had spent here before all hope had died. He wondered if he must go through the same ordeal again.

Professor Millward brushed the snow from the copy of *The Amateur Radio Handbook for 1965*, which had taught him what little he knew about wireless. The test-meters and batteries were still lying in their half-remembered places, and to his relief some of the batteries still held their charge. He searched through the stock until he had built up the necessary power supplies, and checked the radio as well as he could. Then he was ready.

It was a pity that he could never send the manufacturers the testimonial they deserved. The faint 'hiss' from the speaker brought back memories of the BBC, of the nine o'clock news and symphony concerts, of all the things he had taken for granted in a world that was gone like a dream. With scarcely controlled impatience he ran across the wave-bands, but everywhere there was nothing save that omnipresent hiss. That was disappointing, but no more: he remembered that the real test would come at night. In the meantime he would forage among the surrounding shops for anything that might be useful.

It was dusk when he returned to the little room. A hundred miles above his head, tenuous and invisible, the Heaviside Layer would be expanding outwards toward the stars as the sun went down. So it had done every evening for millions of years, and for half a century only, Man had used it for his own purposes, to reflect around the world his messages of hate or peace, to echo with trivialities or to sound with music once called immortal.

Slowly, with infinite patience, Professor Millward began to traverse the shortwave bands that a generation ago had been a babel of shouting voices and stabbing morse. Even as he listened, the faint hope that he had dared to cherish began to fade within him. The city itself was no more silent than the once-crowded oceans of ether. Only the faint crackle of thunderstorms half the world away broke the intolerable stillness. Man had abandoned his latest conquest.

Soon after midnight the batteries faded out. Professor Millward did not have the heart to search for more, but curled up in his furs and fell into a troubled sleep. He got what

18

consolation he could from the thought that if he had not proved his theory, he had not disproved it either.

The heatless sunlight was flooding the lonely white road when he began the homeward journey. He was very tired, for he had slept little, and his sleep had been broken by the recurring fantasy of rescue.

The silence was suddenly broken by the distant thunder that came rolling over the white roofs. It came — there could be no doubt now — from beyond the northern hills that had once been London's playground. From the buildings on either side little avalanches of snow went swishing out into the wide street; then the silence returned.

Professor Millward stood motionless, weighing, considering, analysing. The sound had been too long-drawn out to be an ordinary explosion — he was dreaming again — it was nothing less than the distant thunder of an atomic bomb, burning and blasting away the snow a million tons at a time. His hopes revived, and the disappointments of the night began to fade.

That momentary pause almost cost him his life. Out of a side-street something huge and white moved suddenly into his field of vision. For a moment his mind refused to accept the reality of what he saw; then the paralysis left him and he fumbled desperately for his futile revolver. Padding towards him across the snow, swinging its head from side to side with a hypnotic, serpentine motion, was a huge polar bear.

He dropped his belongings and ran, floundering over the snow towards the nearest buildings. Providentially the Underground entrance was only fifty feet away. The steel grille was closed, but he remembered breaking the lock many years ago. The temptation to look back was almost intolerable, for he could hear nothing to tell how near his pursuer was. For one frightful moment the iron lattice resisted his numbed fingers. Then it yielded reluctantly and he forced his way through the narrow opening.

Out of his childhood there came a sudden incongruous

memory of an albino ferret he had once seen weaving its body ceaselessly across the wire netting of its cage. There was the same reptile grace in the monstrous shape, almost twice as high as a man, that reared itself in baffled fury against the grille. The metal bowed but did not yield beneath the pressure; then the bear dropped to the ground, grunted softly, and padded away. It slashed once or twice at the fallen haversack, scattering a few tins of food into the snow, and vanished as silently as it had come.

A very shaken Professor Millward reached the University three hours later, after moving in short bounds from one refuge to the next. After all these years he was no longer alone in the city. He wondered if there were other visitors, and that same night he knew the answer. Just before dawn he heard, quite distinctly, the cry of a wolf from somewhere in the direction of Hyde Park.

By the end of the week he knew that the animals of the North were on the move. Once he saw a reindeer running southward, pursued by a pack of silent wolves, and sometimes in the night there were sounds of deadly conflict. He was amazed that so much life still existed in the white wilderness between London and the Pole. Now something was driving it southward, and the knowledge brought him a mounting excitement. He did not believe that these fierce survivors would flee from anything save Man.

The strain of waiting was beginning to affect Professor Millward's mind, and for hours he would sit in the cold sunlight, his furs wrapped round him, dreaming of rescue and thinking of the way in which men might be returning to England. Perhaps an expedition had come from North America across the Atlantic ice. It might have been years upon its way. But why had it come so far north? His favourite theory was that the Atlantic ice-packs were not safe enough for heavy traffic farther to the south.

One thing, however, he could not explain to his satisfaction. There had been no air reconnaissance; it was hard to believe

20

that the art of flight had been lost so soon.

Sometimes he would walk along the ranks of books, whispering now and then to a well-loved volume. There were books here that he had not dared to open for years, they reminded him so poignantly of the past. But now, as the days grew longer and brighter, he would sometimes take down a volume of poetry and re-read his old favourites. Then he would go to the tall windows and shout the magic words over the rooftops, as if they would break the spell that had gripped the world.

It was warmer now, as if the ghosts of lost summers had returned to haunt the land. For whole days the temperature rose above freezing, while in many places flowers were breaking through the snow. Whatever was approaching from the north was nearer, and several times a day that enigmatic roar would go thundering over the city, sending the snow sliding upon a thousand roofs.

There were strange, grinding undertones that Professor Millward found baffling and even ominous. At times it was almost as if he were listening to the clash of mighty armies, and sometimes a mad but dreadful thought came into his mind and would not be dismissed. Often he would wake in the night and imagine he heard the sound of mountains moving to the sea.

So the summer wore away, and as the sound of that distant battle drew steadily nearer Professor Millward was the prey of ever more violent alternating hopes and fears. Although he saw no more wolves or bears — they seemed to have fled southward — he did not risk leaving the safety of his fortress. Every morning he would climb to the highest window of the tower and search the northern horizon with field glasses. But all he ever saw was the stubborn retreat of the snows above Hampstead, as they fought their bitter rearguard action against the sun.

His vigil ended with the last days of the brief summer. The grinding thunder in the night had been nearer than ever before, but there was still nothing to hint at its real distance from the city. Professor Millward felt no premonition as he climbed to the narrow window and raised his binoculars to the northern sky.

As a watcher from the walls of some threatened fortress might have seen the first sunlight glinting on the spears of an advancing army, so in that moment Professor Millward knew the truth. The air was crystal-clear, and the hills were sharp and brilliant against the cold blue of the sky. They had lost almost all their snow. Once he would have rejoiced, but it meant nothing now.

Overnight, the enemy he had forgotten had conquered the last defences and was preparing for the final onslaught. As he saw that deadly glitter along the crest of the doomed hills, Professor Millward understood at last the sound he had heard advancing for so many months. It was little wonder he had dreamed of mountains on the march.

Out of the North, their ancient home, returning in triumph to the lands they had once possessed, the glaciers had come again.

The Million Year Picnic

RAY BRADBURY

*Born 1920. American. He began to write short stories for magazines,
after leaving high school, and is now regarded as one of the
best modern science fiction writers.*

Somehow the idea was brought up by Mom that perhaps the
whole family would enjoy a fishing trip. But they weren't Mom's
words; Timothy knew that. They were Dad's words, and Mom
used them for him somehow.

Dad shuffled his feet in a clutter of Martian pebbles and
agreed. So immediately there was a tumult and a shouting, and
very quickly the camp was tucked into capsules and containers,
Mom slipped into travelling jumpers and blouse, Dad stuffed his
pipe full with trembling hands, his eyes on the Martian sky, and
the three boys piled yelling into the motor-boat, none of them
really keeping an eye on Mom and Dad, except Timothy.

Dad pushed a stud. The boat sent a humming sound up into
the sky. The water shook back and the boat nosed ahead, and
the family cried 'Hurrah!'

Timothy sat in the back of the boat with Dad, his small
fingers atop Dad's hairy ones, watching the canal twist, leaving
the crumbled place behind where they had landed in their small
family rocket all the way from Earth. He remembered the night
before they left Earth, the hustling and hurrying, the rocket that
Dad had found somewhere, somehow, and the talk of a vacation
on Mars. A long way to go for a vacation, but Timothy said
nothing because of his younger brothers. They came to Mars
and now, first thing, or so they said, they were going fishing.

Dad had a funny look in his eyes as the boat went up-canal. A
look that Timothy couldn't figure. It was made of strong light
and maybe a sort of relief. It made the deep wrinkles laugh

instead of worry or cry.

So there went the cooling rocket, around a bend, gone.

'How far are we going?' Robert splashed his hand. It looked like a small crab jumping in the violet water.

Dad exhaled. 'A million years.'

'Gee,' said Robert.

'Look, kids.' Mother pointed one soft long arm. 'There's a dead city.'

They looked with fervent anticipation, and the dead city lay dead for them alone, drowsing in a hot silence of summer made on Mars by a Martian weatherman.

And Dad looked as if he was pleased that it was dead.

It was a futile spread of pink rocks sleeping on a rise of sand, a few tumbled pillars, one lonely shrine, and then the sweep of sand again. Nothing else for miles. A white desert around the canal and a blue desert over it.

Just then a bird flew up. Like a stone thrown across a blue pond, hitting, falling deep, and vanishing.

Dad got a frightened look when he saw it, 'I thought it was a rocket.'

Timothy looked at the deep ocean sky, trying to see Earth and the war and the ruined cities and the men killing each other since the day he was born. But he saw nothing. The war was as removed and far off as two flies battling to the death in the arch of a great high and silent cathedral. And just as senseless.

William Thomas wiped his forehead and felt the touch of his son's hand on his arm, like a young tarantula, thrilled. He beamed at his son. 'How goes it, Timmy?'

'Fine, Dad.'

Timothy hadn't quite figured out what was ticking inside the vast adult mechanism beside him. The man with the immense hawk nose, sunburnt, peeling — and the hot blue eyes like agate marbles you play with after school in summer back on Earth, and the long thick columnar legs in the loose riding breeches.

'What are you looking at so hard, Dad?'

24

'I was looking for Earthian logic, common sense, good government, peace, and responsibility.'

'All that up there?'

'No. I didn't find it. It's not there anymore. Maybe it'll never be there again. Maybe we fooled ourselves that it was ever there.'

'Huh?'

'See the fish,' said Dad, pointing.

There rose a soprano clamour from all three boys as they rocked the boat arching their tender necks to see. They *oohed* and *ahed*. A silver ring fish floated by them, undulating, and closing like an iris, instantly, around food particles, to assimilate them.

Dad looked at it. His voice was deep and quiet.

'Just like war. War swims along, sees food, contracts. A moment later — Earth is gone.'

'William,' said Mom.

'Sorry,' said Dad.

They sat still and felt the canal water rush cool, swift and glassy. The only sound was the motor hum, the glide of water, the sun expanding the air.

'When do we see the Martians?' cried Michael.

'Quite soon, perhaps,' said Father. 'Maybe tonight.'

'Oh, but the Martians are a dead race now,' said Mom.

'No, they're not. I'll show you some Martians, all right,' Dad said presently.

Timothy scowled at that but said nothing. Everything was odd now. Vacations and fishing and looks between people.

The other boys were already engaged making shelves of their small hands and peering under them towards the seven-foot stone banks of the canal, watching for Martians.

'What do they look like?' demanded Michael.

'You'll know them when you see them.' Dad sort of laughed, and Timothy saw a pulse beating time in his cheek.

Mother was slender and soft, with a woven plait of spun-gold hair over her head in a tiara, and eyes the colour of the deep cool canal water where it ran in shadow, almost purple with flecks of amber caught in it. You could see her thoughts swimming around in her eyes, like fish — some bright, some dark, some fast, quick, some slow and easy, and sometimes, like when she looked up where Earth was, being colour and nothing else. She sat up in the boat's prow, one hand resting on the side, the other on the lap of her dark blue breeches, and a line of sunburnt soft neck showing where her blouse opened like a white flower.

She kept looking ahead to see what was there, and not being able to see it clearly enough, she looked backwards towards her husband, and through his eyes, reflected there, she saw what was ahead; and since he added part of himself to this reflection, a determined firmness, her face relaxed and she accepted it and she turned back, knowing suddenly what to look for.

Timothy looked too. But all he saw was a straight pencil line of canal going violet through a wide shallow valley penned by low, eroded hills, and on until it fell over the sky's edge. And this canal went on and on, through cities that would have rattled like beetles in a dry skull if you shook them. A hundred or two hundred cities dreaming hot summer-day dreams and cool summer-night dreams . . .

They had come millions of miles for this outing — to fish. But there had been a gun on the rocket. This was a vacation. But why all the food, more than enough to last them years and years, left hidden back there near the rocket? Vacation. Just behind the veil of the vacation was not a soft face of laughter, but something hard and bony and perhaps terrifying. Timothy could not lift the veil, and the two other boys were busy being ten and eight years old, respectively.

'No Martians yet. Nuts.' Robert put his V-shaped chin on his hands and glared at the canal.

Dad had brought an atomic radio along, strapped to his wrist. It functioned on an old-fashioned principle: you held it against the bones near your ear and it vibrated singing or talking to you.

26

Dad listened to it now. His face looked like one of those fallen Martian cities, caved in, sucked dry, almost dead.

Then he gave it to Mom to listen. Her lips dropped open.

'What—' Timothy started to question, but never finished what he wished to say.

For at that moment there were two titanic, marrow-jolting explosions that grew upon themselves, followed by a half dozen minor concussions.

Jerking his head up, Dad notched the boat speed higher immediately. The boat leaped and jounced and spanked. This shook Robert out of his funk and elicited yelps of frightened but ecstatic joy from Michael, who clung to Mom's legs and watched the water pour by his nose in a wet torrent.

Dad swerved the boat, cut speed, and ducked the craft into a little branch canal and under an ancient crumbling stone wharf that smelled of crab flesh. The boat rammed the wharf hard enough to throw them all forward, but no one was hurt, and Dad was already twisted to see if the ripples on the canal were enough to map their route into hiding. Water lines went across, lapped the stones, and rippled back to meet each other, settling, to be dappled by the sun. It all went away.

Dad listened. So did everybody.

Dad's breathing echoed like fists beating against the cold wet wharf stones. In the shadow, Mom's cat eyes just watched Father for some clue to what next.

Dad relaxed and blew out a breath, laughing at himself.

'The rocket, of course. I'm getting jumpy. The rocket.'

Michael said, 'What happened, Dad, what happened?'

'Oh, we just blew up our rocket, is all,' said Timothy, trying to sound matter-of-fact. 'I've heard rockets blown up before. Ours just blew.'

'Why did we blow up our rocket?' asked Michael. 'Huh, Dad?'

'It's part of the game, silly!' said Timothy.

'A game!' Michael and Robert loved the word.

27

'Dad fixed it so it would blow up and no one'd know where we landed or went! In case they ever came looking, see?'

'Oh boy, a secret!'

'Scared by my own rocket,' admitted Dad to Mom. 'I *am* nervous. It's silly to think there'll ever *be* any more rockets. Except *one*, perhaps, if Edwards and his wife get through with *their* ship.'

He put his tiny radio to his ear again. After two minutes he dropped his hand as you would a rag.

'It's over at last,' he said to Mom. 'The radio just went off the atomic beam. Every other world station's gone. They dwindled down to a couple in the last few years. Now the air's completely silent. It'll probably remain silent.'

'For how long?' asked Robert.

'Maybe — your great-grandchildren will hear it again,' said Dad. He just sat there, and the children were caught in the centre of his awe and defeat and resignation and acceptance.

Finally he put the boat out into the canal again, and they continued in the direction in which they had originally started.

It was getting late. Already the sun was down the sky, and a series of dead cities lay ahead of them.

Dad talked very quietly and gently to his sons. Many times in the past he had been brisk, distant, removed from them, but now he patted them on the head with just a word and they felt it.

'Mike, pick a city.'

'What, Dad?'

'Pick a city, son. Any one of these cities we pass.'

'All right,' said Michael. 'How do I pick?'

'Pick the one you like the most. You, too, Robert and Tim. Pick the city you like best.'

'I want a city with Martians in it,' said Michael.

'You'll have that,' said Dad. 'I promise.' His lips were for the children, but his eyes were for Mom.

They passed six cities in twenty minutes. Dad didn't say anything more about the explosions; he seemed much more

28

interested in having fun with his sons, keeping them happy, than anything else.

Michael liked the first city they passed, but this was vetoed because everyone doubted quick first judgements. The second city nobody liked. It was an Earthman's settlement, built of wood and already rotting into sawdust. Timothy liked the third city because it was large. The fourth and fifth were too small and the sixth brought acclaim from everyone, including Mother, who joined in the Gees, Goshes, and Look-at-thats!

There were fifty or sixty huge structures still standing, streets were dusty but paved, and you could see one or two old centrifugal fountains still pulsing wetly in the plazas. That was the only life — water leaping in the late sunlight.

'This is the city,' said everybody.

Steering the boat to a wharf, Dad jumped out.

'Here we are. This is ours. This is where we live from now on!'

'From now on?' Michael was incredulous. He stood up, looking, and then turned to blink back at where the rocket used to be. 'What about the rocket? What about Minnesota?'

'Here,' said Dad.

He touched the small radio to Michael's blond head. 'Listen.'

Michael listened.

'Nothing,' he said.

'That's right. Nothing. Nothing at all any more. No more Minneapolis, no more rockets, no more Earth.'

Michael considered the lethal revelation and began to sob little dry sobs.

'Wait a moment,' said Dad in the next instant. 'I'm giving you a lot more in exchange, Mike!'

'What?' Michael held off the tears, curious, but quite ready to continue in case Dad's further revelation was as disconcerting as the original.

'I'm giving you this city, Mike. It's yours.'

'Mine?'

'For you and Robert and Timothy, all three of you, to own

29

for yourselves.'

Timothy bounded from the boat. 'Look, guys, all for *us!* All of *that!*' He was playing the game with Dad, playing it large and playing it well. Later, after it was all over and things had settled, he could go off by himself and cry for ten minutes. But now it was still a game, still a family outing, and the other kids must be kept playing.

Mike jumped out with Robert. They helped Mom.

'Be careful of your sister,' said Dad, and nobody knew what he meant until later.

They hurried into the great pink-stoned city, whispering among themselves, because dead cities have a way of making you want to whisper, to watch the sun go down.

'In about five days,' said Dad quietly, 'I'll go back down to where our rocket was and collect the food hidden in the ruins there and bring it here; and I'll hunt for Bert Edwards and his wife and daughters there.'

'Daughters?' asked Timothy. 'How many?'

'Four.'

'I can see that'll cause trouble later.' Mom nodded slowly.

'Girls.' Michael made a face like an ancient Martian stone image. 'Girls.'

'Are they coming in a rocket too?'

'Yes. If they make it. Family rockets are made for travel to the Moon, not Mars. We were lucky we got through.'

'Where did you get the rocket?' whispered Timothy, for the other boys were running ahead.

'I saved it. I saved it for twenty years, Tim. I had it hidden away, hoping I'd never have to use it. I suppose I should have given it to the government for the war, but I kept thinking about Mars . . .'

'And a picnic?'

'Right. This is between you and me. When I saw everything was finishing on Earth, after I'd waited until the last moment, I packed us up. Bert Edwards had a ship hidden too, but we decided it would be safer to take off separately, in case anyone tried to shoot us down.'

'Why'd you blow up the rocket, Dad?'

'So we can't go back, ever. And so if any of those evil men ever come to Mars they won't know we're here.'

'Is that why you look up all the time?'

'Yes, it's silly. They won't follow us, ever. They haven't anything to follow with. I'm being too careful, is all.'

Michael came running back. 'Is this really *our* city, Dad?'

'The whole darn planet belongs to us, kids. The whole darn planet.'

They stood there, King of the Hill, Top of the Heap, Ruler of All They Surveyed, Unimpeachable Monarchs and Presidents, trying to understand what it meant to own a world and how big a world really was.

Night came quickly in the thin atmosphere, and Dad left them in the square by the pulsing fountain, went down to the boat, and came walking back carrying a stack of paper in his big hands.

He laid the papers in a clutter in an old courtyard and set them afire. To keep warm, they crouched around the blaze and laughed, and Timothy saw the little letters leap like frightened animals when the flames touched and engulfed them. The papers crinkled like an old man's skin, and the cremation surrounded innumerable words:

'GOVERNMENT BONDS; Business Graph, 1999; Religious Prejudice: An Essay; The Science of Logistics; Problems of the Pan-American Unity; Stock Report for July 3, 1998; The War Digest . . .'

Dad had insisted on bringing these papers for this purpose. He sat there and fed them into the fire, one by one, with satisfaction, and told his children what it all meant.

'It's time I told you a few things. I don't suppose it was fair, keeping so much from you. I don't know if you'll understand, but I have to talk, even if only part of it gets over to you.'

31

He dropped a leaf in the fire.

'I'm burning a way of life, just like that way of life is being burned clean off Earth right now. Forgive me if I talk like a politician. I am, after all, a former state governor, and I was honest and they hated me for it. Life on Earth never settled down to doing anything very good. Science ran too far ahead of us too quickly, and the people got lost in a mechanical wilderness, like children making over pretty things, gadgets, helicopters, rockets; emphasizing the wrong items, emphasizing machines instead of how to run the machines. Wars got bigger and bigger and finally killed Earth. That's what the silent radio means. That's what we ran away from.

'We were lucky. There aren't any more rockets left. It's time you knew this isn't a fishing trip at all. I put off telling you. Earth is gone. Interplanetary travel won't be back for centuries, maybe never. But that way of life proved itself wrong, and strangled itself with its own hands. You're young. I'll tell you this again every day until it sinks in.'

He paused to feed more papers to the fire.

'Now we're alone. We and a handful of others who'll land in a few days. Enough to start over. Enough to turn away from all that back on Earth and strike out on a new line—'

The fire leaped up to emphasize his talking. And then all the papers were gone except one. All the laws and beliefs of Earth were burnt into small hot ashes which soon would be carried off in a wind.

Timothy looked at the last thing that Dad tossed in the fire. It was a map of the World, and it wrinkled and distorted itself hotly and went — flimpf — and was gone like a warm, black butterfly. Timothy turned away.

'Now I'm going to show you the Martians,' said Dad. 'Come on, all of you. Here, Alice,' He took her hand.

Michael was crying loudly, and Dad picked him up and carried him, and they walked down through the ruins towards the canal.

The canal. Where tomorrow or the next day their future wives would come up in a boat, small laughing girls now, with their father and mother.

The night came down around them, and there were stars. But Timothy couldn't find Earth. It had already set. That was something to think about.

A night bird called among the ruins as they walked. Dad said, 'Your mother and I will try to teach you. Perhaps we'll fail. I hope not. We've had a good lot to see and learn from. We planned this trip years ago, before you were born. Even if there hadn't been a war we would have come to Mars, I think, to live and form our own standard of living. It would have been another century before Mars would have been really poisoned by the Earth civilization. Now, of course—'

They reached the canal. It was long and straight and cool and wet and reflective in the night.

'I've always wanted to see a Martian,' said Michael. 'Where are they, Dad? You promised.'

'There they are,' said Dad, and he shifted Michael on his shoulder and pointed straight down.

The Martians were there. Timothy began to shiver.

The Martians were there — in the canal — reflected in the water. Timothy and Michael and Robert and Mom and Dad.

The Martians stared back up at them for a long, long silent time from the rippling water . . .

Compassion Circuit

JOHN WYNDHAM

1903-1969. British. Achieved success in 1951 with The Day of
the Triffids, *which was followed by a number of
science fiction works, which he called 'logical fantasies'.*

By the time Janet had been five days in hospital she had become
converted to the idea of a domestic robot. It had taken her two
days to discover that Nurse James *was* a robot, one day to get
over the surprise, and two more to realize what a comfort an
attendant robot could be.

The conversion was a relief. Practically every house she visited
had a domestic robot; it was the family's second or third most
valuable possession — the women tended to rate it slightly
higher than the car; the men, slightly lower. Janet had been
perfectly well aware for some time that her friends regarded her
as a nitwit or worse for wearing herself out with looking after a
house which a robot would be able to keep spick and span with
a few hours' work a day. She had also known that it irritated
George to come home each evening to a wife who had tired
herself out by unnecessary work. But the prejudice had been
firmly set. It was not the diehard attitude of people who refused
to be served by robot waiters, or driven by robot drivers (who,
incidentally, were much safer), led by robot shop-guides, or see
dresses modelled by robot mannequins. It was simply an
uneasiness about them, and being left alone with one — and a
disinclination to feel such an uneasiness in her own home.

She herself attributed the feeling largely to the conservatism
of her own home which had used no house-robots. Other people,
who had been brought up in homes run by robots, even the
primitive types available a generation before, never seemed to
have such a feeling at all. It irritated her to know that her

34

husband thought she was *afraid* of them in a childish way. That, she had explained to George a number of times, was not so, and was not the point, either: what she did dislike was the idea of one intruding upon her personal, domestic life, which was what a house-robot was bound to do.

The robot who was called Nurse James was, then, the first with which she had ever been in close personal contact and she, or it, came as a revelation.

Janet told the doctor of her enlightenment, and he looked relieved. She also told George when he looked in in the afternoon: he was delighted. The two of them conferred before he left the hospital. 'Excellent,' said the doctor. 'To tell you the truth I was afraid we were up against a real neurosis there — and very inconveniently, too. Your wife can never have been strong, and in the last few years she's worn herself out running the house.'

'I know,' George agreed. 'I tried hard to persuade her during the first two years we were married, but it only led to trouble so I had to drop it. This is really a culmination — she was rather shaken when she found that the reason she'd have to come here was partly because there was no robot at home to look after her.'

'Well, there's one thing certain, she can't go on as she has been doing. If she tries to she'll be back here inside a couple of months,' the doctor told him.

'She won't now. She's really changed her mind,' George assured him. 'Part of the trouble was that she's never come across a really modern one, except in a superficial way. The newest that any of our friends has is ten years old at least, and most of them are older than that. She'd never contemplated the idea of anything as advanced as Nurse James. The question now is what pattern?'

The doctor thought a moment.

'Frankly, Mr Shand, your wife is going to need a lot of rest and looking after, I'm afraid. What I'd really recommend for her is the type they have here. It's something pretty new, this

35

Nurse James model. A specially developed high-sensibility job with a quite novel contra-balanced compassion-protection circuit — a very tricky bit of work that. Any direct order which a normal robot would obey at once is evaluated by the circuit, it is weighed against the benefit or harm to the patient and, unless it is beneficial, or at least harmless, to the patient, it is not obeyed. They've proved to be wonderful for nursing and looking after children — but there is a big demand for them, and I'm afraid they're pretty expensive.'

'How much?' asked George.

The doctor's round-figure price made him frown for a moment. Then he said: 'It'll make a hole, but, after all, it's mostly Janet's economies and simple-living that's built up the savings. Where do I get one?'

'You don't. Not just like that,' the doctor told him. 'I shall have to throw a bit of weight about for a priority, but in the circumstances I shall get it, all right. Now, you go and fix up the details of appearance and so on with your wife. Let me know how she wants it, and I'll get busy.'

*   *   *

'A proper one,' said Janet. 'One that'll look right in a house, I mean. I couldn't do with one of those levers-and-plastic box things that stare at you with lenses. As it's got to look after the house, let's have it looking like a housemaid.'

'Or a houseman, if you like?'

She shook her head. 'No. It's going to have to look after me, too, so I think I'd rather it was a housemaid. It can have a black silk dress and a frilly white apron and a cap. And I'd like it blonde — a sort of darkish blonde — and about five feet ten, and nice to look at, but not *too* beautiful. I don't want to be jealous of it . . .'

*   *   *

The doctor kept Janet ten days more in the hospital while the

36

matter was settled. There had been luck in coming in for a cancelled order, but inevitably some delay while it was adapted to Janet's specification — also it had required the addition of standard domestic pseudo-memory patterns to suit it for house-work.

It was delivered the day after she got back. Two severely functional robots carried the case up the front path, and inquired whether they should unpack it. Janet thought not, and told them to leave it in the outhouse.

When George got back he wanted to open it at once, but Janet shook her head.

'Supper first,' she decided. 'A robot doesn't mind waiting.'

Nevertheless it was a brief meal. When it was over, George carried the dishes out and stacked them in the sink.

'No more washing-up,' he said, with satisfaction.

He went out to borrow the next-door robot to help him carry the case in. Then he found his end of it more than he could lift, and had to borrow the robot from the house opposite, too. Presently the pair of them carried it in and laid it on the kitchen floor as if it were a featherweight, and went away again.

George got out the screwdriver and drew the six large screws that held the lid down. Inside there was a mass of shavings. He shoved them out, on to the floor. Janet protested.

'What's the matter? *We* shan't have to clear up,' he said, happily.

There was an inner case of wood pulp, with a snowy layer of wadding under its lid. George rolled it up and pushed it out of the way, and there, ready dressed in black frock and white apron, lay the robot.

They regarded it for some seconds without speaking.

It was remarkably lifelike. For some reason it made Janet feel a little queer to realize that it was *her* robot — a trifle nervous, and, obscurely, a trifle guilty . . .

'Sleeping beauty,' remarked George, reaching for the instruction book on its chest.

In point of fact the robot was not a beauty. Janet's preference had been observed. It was pleasant and nice-looking without being striking, but the details were good. The deep gold hair was quite enviable — although one knew that it was probably threads of plastic with waves that would never come out. The skin — another kind of plastic covering the carefully built-up contours — was distinguishable from real skin only by its perfection.

Janet knelt down beside the box, and ventured a forefinger to touch the flawless complexion. It was quite, quite cold.

She sat back on her heels, looking at it. Just a big doll, she told herself; a contraption, a very wonderful contraption of metal, plastics, and electronic circuits, but still a contraption, and made to look as it did simply because people, including herself, would find it harsh or grotesque if it should look any other way . . . And yet, to have it looking as it did was a bit disturbing, too, For one thing, you couldn't go on thinking of it as 'it' any more; whether you liked it or not, your mind thought of it as 'her'. As 'her' it would have to have a name; and with a name, it would become still more of a person.

'"A battery-driven model,"' George read out, '"will normally require to be fitted with a new battery every four days. Other models, however, are designed to conduct their own regeneration from the mains as and when necessary." Let's have her out.'

He put his hands under the robot's shoulders, and tried to lift it.

'Phew!' he said. 'Must be about three times my weight.' He had another try. 'Hell,' he said, and referred to the book again.

'"The control switches are situated at the back, slightly above the waistline." All right, maybe we can roll her over.'

With an effort he succeeded in getting the figure on to its side and began to undo the buttons at the back of her dress. Janet suddenly felt that to be an indelicacy. 'I'll do it,' she said.

Her husband glanced at her.

'All right. It's yours,' he told her.

38

'She can't be just "it". I'm going to call her Hester.'

'All right, again,' he agreed.

Janet undid the buttons and fumbled about inside the dress.

'I can't find a knob, or anything,' she said.

'Apparently there's a small panel that opens,' he told her.

'Oh, no!' she said, in a slightly shocked tone.

He regarded her again.

'Darling, she's just a robot; a mechanism.'

'I know,' said Janet, shortly. She felt about again, discovered the panel, and opened it.

'You give the upper knob a half-turn to the right and then close the panel to complete the circuit,' instructed George, from the book.

Janet did so, and then sat swiftly back on her heels again, watching.

The robot stirred and turned. It sat up, then it got to its feet. It stood before them, looking the very pattern of a stage parlourmaid. 'Good day, madam,' it said. 'Good day, sir. I shall be happy to serve you.'

*   *   *

'Thank you, Hester,' Janet said, as she leaned back against the cushion placed behind her. Not that it was necessary to thank a robot, but she had a theory that if you did not practise politeness with robots you soon forgot it with other people.

And, anyway, Hester was no ordinary robot. She was not even dressed as a parlourmaid any more. In four months she had become a friend, a tireless, attentive friend. From the first Janet had found it difficult to believe that she was only a mechanism, and as the days passed she had become more and more of a person. The fact that she consumed electricity instead of food came to seem little more than a foible. The time she couldn't stop walking in a circle, and the other time when something went wrong with her vision so that she did everything a foot to the right of where she ought to have been doing it, these things were just indispositions such as anyone might have, and the robot-mechanic who came to adjust her paid his call much like any other doctor. Hester was not only a person; she was preferable company to many.

'I suppose,' said Janet, settling back in her chair, 'that you must think me a poor, weak thing?'

What one must not expect from Hester was euphemism.

'Yes,' she said, directly. But then she added: 'I think all humans are poor, weak things. It is the way they are made. One must be sorry for them.'

Janet had long ago given up thinking things like: 'That'll be the compassion-circuit speaking,' or trying to imagine the computing, selecting, associating, and shunting that must be going on to produce such a remark. She took it as she might from — well, say, a foreigner. She said:

'Compared with robots we must seem so, I suppose. You are so strong and untiring, Hester. If you knew how I envy you that . .'

Hester said, matter of factly: 'We were designed: you were just accidental. It is your misfortune, not your fault.'

'You'd rather be you than me?' asked Janet.

'Certainly,' Hester told her. 'We are stronger. We don't have to have frequent sleep to recuperate. We don't have to carry an unreliable chemical factory inside us. We don't have to grow old and deteriorate. Human beings are so clumsy and fragile and so often unwell because something is not working properly. If anything goes wrong with us, or is broken, it doesn't hurt and is easily replaced. And you have all kinds of words like pain, and suffering, and unhappiness, and weariness that we have to be taught to understand, and they don't seem to us to be useful things to have. I feel sorry that you must have these things and be so uncertain and so fragile. It disturbs my compassion-circuit.'

'Uncertain and fragile,' Janet repeated. 'Yes, that's how I feel.'

'Humans have to live so precariously,' Hester went on. 'If my arm or leg should be crushed I can have a new one in a few minutes, but a human would have agony for a long time, and not even a new limb at the end of it — just a faulty one, if he is lucky. That isn't as bad as it used to be because in designing us you learned how to make good arms and legs, much stronger and better than the old ones. People would be much more sensible to have a weak arm or leg replaced at once, but they don't seem to want to if they can possibly keep the old ones.'

'You mean they can be grafted on? I didn't know that,' Janet said. 'I wish it were only arms or legs that's wrong with me. I don't think I would hesitate. . .' She sighed. 'The doctor wasn't encouraging this morning, Hester. You heard what he said? I've been losing ground: must rest more. I don't believe he does expect me to get any stronger. He was just trying to cheer me up before . . . He had a funny sort of look after he'd examined me . . . But all he said was rest. What's the good of being alive if it's only rest — rest — rest . . .? And there's poor George. What sort of life is it for him, and he's so patient with me, so sweet . . . I'd rather anything than go on feebly like this. I'd sooner die . . .'

Janet went on talking, more to herself than to the patient Hester standing by. She talked herself into tears. Then, presently, she looked up.

'Oh, Hester, if you were human I couldn't bear it; I think I'd hate you for being so strong and so well — but I don't, Hester. You're so kind and so patient when I'm silly, like this. I believe you'd cry with me to keep me company if you could.'

'I would if I could,' the robot agreed. 'My compassion-circuit —'

'Oh, no!' Janet protested. 'It can't be just that. You've a heart somewhere, Hester. You must have.'

'I expect it is more reliable than a heart,' said Hester.

She stepped a little closer, stooped down, and lifted Janet up as if she weighed nothing at all.

'You've tired yourself out, Janet dear,' she told her. 'I'll take you upstairs; you'll be able to sleep a little before he gets back.'

41

Janet could feel the robot's arms cold through her dress, but the coldness did not trouble her any more, she was aware only that they were strong, protecting arms around her. She said:

'Oh, Hester, you are such a comfort, you *know* what I ought to do.' She paused, then she added miserably: 'I know what he thinks — the doctor, I mean. I could see it. He just thinks I'm going to go on getting weaker and weaker until one day I'll fade away and die . . . I said I'd sooner die . . . but I wouldn't, Hester. I don't want to die . . .'

The robot rocked her a little, as if she were a child.

'There, there, dear. It's not as bad as that — nothing like,' she told her. 'You mustn't think about dying. And you mustn't cry any more, it's not good for you, you know. Besides, you don't want him to see you've been crying.'

'I'll try not to,' agreed Janet obediently, as Hester carried her out of the room and up the stairs.

*   *   *

The hospital reception-robot looked up from the desk.

'My wife,' George said, 'I rang you up about an hour ago.'

The robot's face took on an impeccable expression of professional sympathy.

'Yes, Mr Shand. I'm afraid it has been a shock for you, but as I told you, your house-robot did quite the right thing to send her here at once.'

'I've tried to get on to her own doctor, but he's away,' George told her.

'You don't need to worry about that, Mr Shand. She has been examined, and we have had all her records sent over from the hospital she was in before. The operation has been provisionally fixed for tomorrow, but of course we shall need your consent.'

George hesitated. 'May I see the doctor in charge of her?'

'He isn't in the hospital at the moment, I'm afraid.'

'Is it — absolutely necessary?' George asked after a pause.

The robot looked at him steadily, and nodded.

'She must have been growing steadily weaker for some months now,' she said. George nodded.

'The only alternative is that she will grow weaker still, and have more pain before the end,' she told him.

George stared at the wall blankly for some seconds.

'I see,' he said bleakly.

He picked up a pen in a shaky hand and signed the form that she put before him. He gazed at it a while without seeing it.

'She'll — she'll have — a good chance?' he asked.

'Yes,' the robot told him. 'There is never complete absence of risk, of course, but she has a better than seventy-per-cent likelihood of complete success.'

George sighed, and nodded. 'I'd like to see her,' he said.

The robot pressed a bell-push.

'You may *see* her,' she said. 'But I must ask you not to disturb her. She's asleep now, and it's better for her not to be woken.'

George had to be satisfied with that, but he left the hospital feeling a little better for the sight of the quiet smile on Janet's lips as she slept.

*   *   *

The hospital called him at the office the following afternoon. They were reassuring. The operation appeared to have been a complete success. Everyone was quite confident of the outcome. There was no need to worry. The doctors were perfectly satisfied. No, it would not be wise to allow any visitors for a few days yet. But there was nothing to worry about. Nothing at all.

George rang up each day just before he left, in the hope that he would be allowed to visit. The hospital was kindly and heartening, but adamant about visits. And then, on the fifth day, they suddenly told him she had left on her way home. George was staggered: he had been prepared to find it a matter of weeks. He dashed out, bought a bunch of roses, and left half a dozen traffic regulations in fragments behind him. 'Where is she?' he demanded of Hester as she opened the door.

43

'She's in bed. I thought it might be better if — ' Hester began, but he lost the rest of the sentence as he bounded up the stairs.

Janet was lying in the bed. Only her head was visible, cut off by the line of the sheet and a bandage round her neck. George put the flowers down on the bedside table. He stooped over Janet and kissed her gently. She looked up at him from anxious eyes.

'Oh, George dear. Has she told you?'

'Has who told me what?' he asked, sitting down on the side of the bed.

'Hester. She said she would. Oh, George, I didn't mean it, at least I don't think I meant it . . . She sent me, George. I was so weak and wretched. I wanted to be strong. I don't think I really understood. Hester said —'

'Take it easy, darling. Take it easy,' George suggested with a smile. 'What on earth's all this about?'

He felt under the bedclothes and found her hand.

'But, George —' she began. He interrupted her.

'I say, darling, your hand's dreadfully cold. It's almost like —' His fingers slid further up her arm. His eyes widened at her, incredulously. He jumped up suddenly from the bed and flung back the covers. He put his hand on the thin nightdress, over her heart — and then snatched it away as if he had been stung. 'God — NO! — ' he said, staring at her.

'But George. George, darling —' said Janet's head on the pillows.

'NO — NO!' cried George, almost in a shriek.

He turned and ran blindly from the room.

In the darkness on the landing he missed the top step of the stairs, and went headlong down the whole flight.

*   *   *

Hester found him lying in a huddle in the hall. She bent down and gently explored the damage. The extent of it, and the fragility of the frame that had suffered it disturbed her compassion-circuit very greatly. She did not try to move him, but went to the telephone and dialled.

'Emergency?' she asked, and gave the name and address. 'Yes at once,' she told them. 'There may not be a lot of time. Several compound fractures, and I think his back is broken, poor man. No. There appears to be no damage to his head. Yes, much better. He'd be crippled for life, even if he did get over it . . . Yes, better send the form of consent with the ambulance so that it can be signed at once . . . Oh, yes, that'll be quite all right. His wife will sign it.'

Robbie

ISAAC ASIMOV

*Born 1920. American. Assoc. Prof. of Biochemistry. Best known
as the author of* Nightfall, *which has become a classic.
The 'father' of modern science fiction.*

'Ninety-eight — ninety-nine — *one hundred.'* Gloria
withdrew her chubby little forearm from before her eyes and
stood for a moment, wrinkling her nose and blinking in the
sunlight. Then, trying to watch in all directions at once, she
withdrew a few cautious steps from the tree against which she
had been leaning.

She craned her neck to investigate the possibilities of a clump
of bushes to the right and then withdrew farther to obtain a
better angle for viewing its dark recesses. The quiet was
profound except for the incessant buzzing of insects and the
occasional chirrup of some hardy bird, braving the midday sun.

Gloria pouted, 'I bet he went inside the house, and I've told
him a million times that that's not fair.'

With tiny lips pressed together tightly and a severe frown
crinkling her forehead, she moved determinedly towards the
two-storey building up past the driveway.

Too late she heard the rustling sound behind her, followed by
the distinctive and rhythmic clump-clump of Robbie's metal feet.
She whirled about to see her triumphing companion emerge
from hiding and make for the home-tree at full speed.

Gloria shrieked in dismay. 'Wait, Robbie! That wasn't fair,
Robbie! You promised you wouldn't run until I found you.' Her
little feet could make no headway at all against Robbie's giant
strides. Then, within ten feet of the goal, Robbie's pace slowed
suddenly to the merest of crawls, and Gloria, with one final
burst of wild speed, dashed pantingly past him to touch the

welcome bark of home-tree first.

Gleefully, she turned on the faithful Robbie, and with the basest of ingratitude, rewarded him for his sacrifice, by taunting him cruelly for a lack of running ability.

'Robbie can't run,' she shouted at the top of her eight-year-old voice. 'I can beat him any day. I can beat him any day.' She chanted the words in a shrill rhythm.

Robbie didn't answer, of course — not in words. He pantomimed running, instead, inching away until Gloria found herself running after him as he dodged her narrowly, forcing her to veer in helpless circles, little arms outstretched and fanning at the air.

'Robbie,' she squealed, 'stand still!' — And the laughter was forced out of her in breathless jerks.

— Until he turned suddenly and caught her up, whirling her round, so that for her the world fell away for a moment with a blue emptiness beneath, and green trees stretching hungrily downward towards the void. Then she was down in the grass again, leaning against Robbie's leg and still holding a hard, metal finger.

After a while, her breath returned. She pushed uselessly at her disheveled hair in vague imitation of one of her mother's gestures and twisted to see if her dress were torn.

She slapped her hand against Robbie's torso, 'Bad boy! I'll spank you!'

And Robbie cowered, holding his hands over his face so that she had to add, 'No, I won't, Robbie. I won't spank you. But anyway, it's my turn to hide now because you've got longer legs and you promised not to run till I found you.'

Robbie nodded his head — a small parallelepiped with rounded edges and corners attached to a similar but much larger parallelepiped that served as torso by means of a short, flexible stalk — and obediently faced the tree. A thin, metal film descended over his glowing eyes and from within his body came a steady, resonant ticking.

47

'Don't peek now — and don't skip any numbers,' warned Gloria, and scurried for cover.

With unvarying regularity, seconds were ticked off, and at the hundredth, up went the eyelids, and the glowing red of Robbie's eyes swept the prospect. They rested for a moment on a bit of colourful gingham that protruded from behind a boulder. He advanced a few steps and convinced himself that it was Gloria who squatted behind it.

Slowly, remaining always between Gloria and home-tree, he advanced on the hiding place, and when Gloria was plainly in sight and could no longer even theorize to herself that she was not seen, he extended one arm toward her, slapping the other against his leg so that it rang again. Gloria emerged sulkily.

'You peeked!' she exclaimed, with gross unfairness. 'Besides I'm tired of playing hide-and-seek. I want a ride.'

But Robbie was hurt at the unjust accusation, so he seated himself carefully and shook his head ponderously from side to side.

Gloria changed her tone to one of gentle coaxing immediately, 'Come on, Robbie. I didn't mean it about the peeking. Give me a ride.'

Robbie was not to be won over so easily, though. He gazed stubbornly at the sky, and shook his head even more emphatically.

'Please, Robbie, please give me a ride.' She encircled his neck with rosy arms and hugged tightly. Then, changing moods in a moment, she moved away. 'If you don't, I'm going to cry,' and her face twisted appallingly in preparation.

Hard-hearted Robbie paid scant attention to this dreadful possibility, and shook his head a third time. Gloria found it necessary to play her trump card.

'If you don't,' she exclaimed warmly, 'I won't tell you any more stories, that's all. Not one —'

Robbie gave in immediately and unconditionally before this ultimatum, nodding his head vigorously until the metal of his neck hummed. Carefully, he raised the little girl and placed her on his broad, flat shoulders.

Gloria's threatened tears vanished immediately and she crowed with delight. Robbie's metal skin, kept at a constant temperature of seventy by the high resistance coils within felt nice and comfortable, while the beautifully loud sound her heels made as they bumped rhythmically against his chest was enchanting.

'You're an air-coaster, Robbie, you're a big, silver air-coaster. Hold out your arms straight. — You *got* to, Robbie, if you're going to be an air-coaster.'

The logic was irrefutable. Robbie's arms were wings catching the air currents and he was a silver'coaster.

Gloria twisted the robot's head and leaned to the right. He banked sharply. Gloria equipped the 'coaster with a motor that went 'Br-r-r' and then with weapons that went 'Powie' and 'Sh-sh-shshsh.' Pirates were giving chase and the ship's blasters were coming into play. The pirates dropped in a steady rain.

'Got another one. — Two more,' she cried.

Then 'Faster, men,' Gloria said pompously, 'we're running out of ammunition.' She aimed over her shoulder with undaunted courage and Robbie was a blunt-nosed spaceship zooming through the void at maximum acceleration.

Clear across the field he sped, to the patch of tall grass on the other side, where he stopped with a suddenness that evoked a shriek from his flushed rider, and then tumbled her on to the soft, green carpet.

Gloria gasped and panted, and gave voice to intermittent whispered exclamations of 'That was *nice*!'

Robbie waited until she had caught her breath and then pulled gently at a lock of hair.

'You want something?' said Gloria, eyes wide in an apparently artless complexity that fooled her huge 'nursemaid' not at all. He pulled the curl harder.

'Oh, I know. You want a story.'

49

Robbie nodded rapidly.

'Which one?'

Robbie made a semi-circle in the air with one finger.

The little girl protested, 'Again? I've told you Cinderella a million times. Aren't you tired of it? — It's for babies.'

Another semi-circle.

'Oh, hell,' Gloria composed herself, ran over the details of the tale in her mind (together with her own elaborations, of which she had several) and began:

'Are you ready? Well — once upon a time there was a beautiful little girl whose name was Ella. And she had a terribly cruel step-mother and two very ugly and *very* cruel step-sisters and —'

*   *   *

Gloria was reaching the very climax of the tale — midnight was striking and everything was changing back to the shabby originals lickety-split, while Robbie listened tensely with burning eyes — when the interruption came.

'Gloria!'

It was the high-pitched sound of a woman who has been calling not once, but several times; and had the nervous tone of one in whom anxiety was beginning to overcome impatience.

'Mamma's calling me,' said Gloria, not quite happily. 'You'd better carry me back to the house, Robbie.'

Robbie obeyed with alacrity for somehow there was that in him which judged it best to obey Mrs Weston, without as much as a scrap of hesitation. Gloria's father was rarely home in the daytime except on Sunday — today, for instance — and when he was, he proved a genial and understanding person. Gloria's mother, however, was a source of uneasiness to Robbie and there was always the impulse to sneak away from her sight.

Mrs Weston caught sight of them the minute they rose above the masking tufts of long grass and retired inside the house to wait.

'I've shouted myself hoarse, Gloria,' she said, severely. 'Where were you?'

'I was with Robbie,' quavered Gloria. 'I was telling him Cinderella, and I forgot it was dinner-time.'

'Well, it's a pity Robbie forgot, too.' Then, as if that reminded her of the robot's presence, she whirled upon him. 'You may go, Robbie. She doesn't need you now.' Then, brutally, 'And don't come back till I call you.'

Robbie turned to go, but hesitated as Gloria cried out in his defense, 'Wait, Mamma, you got to let him stay. I didn't finish Cinderella for him. I said I would tell him Cinderella and I'm not finished.'

'Gloria!'

'Honest and truly, Mamma, he'll stay so quiet, you won't even know he's here. He can sit on the chair in the corner, and he won't say a word, — I mean he won't *do* anything. Will you, Robbie?'

Robbie, appealed to, nodded his massive head up and down once.

'Gloria, if you don't stop this at once, you shan't see Robbie for a whole week.'

The girl's eyes fell, 'All right! But Cinderella is his favourite story and I didn't finish it. — And he likes it so much.'

The robot left with a disconsolate step and Gloria choked back a sob.

*   *   *

George Weston was comfortable. It was a habit of his to be comfortable on Sunday afternoons. A good, hearty dinner below the hatches; a nice, soft, dilapidated couch on which to sprawl; a copy of the *Times;* slippered feet and shirtless chest; — how could anyone *help* but be comfortable?

He wasn't pleased, therefore, when his wife walked in. After ten years of married life, he still was so unutterably foolish as to love her, and there was no question that he was always glad to see her — still Sunday afternoons just after dinner were sacred to him and his idea of solid comfort was to be left in utter solitude for two or three hours. Consequently, he fixed his eye firmly upon the latest reports of the Lefebre-Yoshida expedition to Mars (this one was to take off from Lunar Base and might actually succeed) and pretended she wasn't there.

Mrs Weston waited patiently for two minutes, then impatiently for two more, and finally broke the silence.

'George!'

'Hmpph?'

'George, I say! *Will* you put down that paper and look at me?'

The paper rustled to the floor and Weston turned a weary face toward his wife, 'What is it, dear?'

'You know what it is, George. It's Gloria and that terrible machine.'

'What terrible machine?'

'Now don't pretend you don't know what I'm talking about. It's that robot Gloria calls Robbie. He doesn't leave her for a moment.'

'Well, why should he? He's not supposed to. And he certainly isn't a terrible machine. He's the best darn robot money can buy and I'm damned sure he set me back half a year's income. He's worth it, though — darn sight cleverer than half my office staff.'

He made a move to pick up the paper again, but his wife was quicker and snatched it away.

'You listen to *me*, George. I won't have my daughter entrusted to a machine — and I don't care how clever it is. It has no soul, and no one knows what it may be thinking. A child just isn't *made* to be guarded by a thing of metal.'

Weston frowned, 'When did you decide this? He's been with Gloria two years now and I haven't seen you worry till now.'

'It was different at first. It was a novelty; it took a load off me, and — and it was a fashionable thing to do. But now I don't know. The neighbours —'

'Well, what have the neighbours to do with it. Now, look. A robot is infinitely more to be trusted than a human nursemaid.

52

Robbie was constructed for only one purpose really — to be the companion of a little child. His entire "mentality" has been created for the purpose. He just can't help being faithful and loving and kind. He's a machine — *made so*. That's more than you can say for humans.'

'But something might go wrong. Some — some —' Mrs Weston was a bit hazy about the insides of a robot, 'some little jigger will come loose and the awful thing will go berserk and — and —' She couldn't bring herself to complete the quite obvious thought.

'Nonsense,' Weston denied, with an involuntary nervous shiver. 'That's completely ridiculous. We had a long discussion at the time we bought Robbie about the First Law of Robotics. You *know* that it is impossible for a robot to harm a human being; that long before enough can go wrong to alter that First Law, a robot would be completely inoperable. It's a mathematical impossibility. Besides I have an engineer from U S Robots here twice a year to give the poor gadget a complete overhaul. Why, there's no more chance of anything at all going wrong with Robbie than there is of you or I suddenly going looney — considerably less, in fact. Besides, how are you going to take him away from Gloria?'

He made another futile stab at the paper and his wife tossed it angrily into the next room.

'That's just it, George! She won't play with anyone else. There are dozens of little boys and girls that she should make friends with, but she won't. She won't go *near* them unless I make her. That's no way for a little girl to grow up. You want her to be normal, don't you? You want her to be able to take her part in society.'

'You're jumping at shadows, Grace. Pretend Robbie's a dog. I've seen hundreds of children who would rather have their dog than their father.'

'A dog is different, George. We *must* get rid of that horrible thing. You can sell it back to the company. I've asked, and you can.'

'You've *asked*? Now look here, Grace, let's not go off the deep end. We're keeping the robot until Gloria is older and I don't want the subject brought up again.' And with that he walked out of the room in a huff.

*   *   *

Mrs Weston met her husband at the door two evenings later. 'You'll have to listen to this, George. There's bad feeling in the village.'

'About what?' asked Weston. He stepped into the washroom and drowned out any possible answer by the splash of water.

Mrs Weston waited. She said, 'About Robbie.'

Weston stepped out, towel in hand, face red and angry. 'What are you talking about?'

'Oh, it's been building up and building up. I've tried to close my eyes to it, but I'm not going to any more. Most of the villagers consider Robbie dangerous. Children aren't allowed to go near our place in the evenings.'

'We trust *our* child with the thing.'

'Well, people aren't reasonable about these things.'

'Then to hell with them.'

'Saying that doesn't solve the problem. I've got to do my shopping down there. I've got to meet them every day. And it's even worse in the city these days when it comes to robots. New York has just passed an ordinance keeping all robots off the streets between sunset and sunrise.'

'All right, but they can't stop us from keeping a robot in our home. — Grace, this is one of your campaigns. I recognize it. But it's no use. The answer is still, no! We're keeping Robbie!'

*   *   *

And yet he loved his wife — and what was worse, his wife knew it. George Weston, after all, was only a man — poor thing — and his wife made full use of every device which a clumsier and

54

more scrupulous sex has learned, with reason and futility, to fear.

Ten times in the ensuing week, he cried, 'Robbie stays, — and that's *final*!' and each time it was weaker and accompanied by a louder and more agonized groan.

Came the day at last, when Weston approached his daughter guiltily and suggested a 'beautiful' visivox show in the village.

Gloria clapped her hands happily, 'Can Robbie go?'

'No, dear,' he said, and winced at the sound of his voice, 'they won't allow robots at the visivox — but you can tell him all about it when you get home.' He stumbled all over the last few words and looked away.

Gloria came back from town bubbling over with enthusiasm, for the visivox had been a gorgeous spectacle indeed.

She waited for her father to manoeuvre the jet-car into the sunken garage, 'Wait till I tell Robbie, Daddy. He would have liked it like anything. —Especially when Francis Fran was backing away so-o-o quietly, and backed right into one of the Leopard-Men and had to run.' She laughed again. 'Daddy, are there really Leopard-Men on the Moon?'

'Probably not,' said Weston absently. 'It's just funny make-believe.' He couldn't take much longer with the car. He'd have to face it.

Gloria ran across the lawn. 'Robbie. — Robbie!'

Then she stopped suddenly at the sight of a beautiful collie which regarded her out of serious brown eyes as it wagged its tail on the porch.

'Oh, what a nice dog!' Gloria climbed the steps, approached cautiously and patted it. 'Is it for me, Daddy?'

Her mother had joined them. 'Yes, it is Gloria. Isn't it nice — soft and furry. It's very gentle. It *likes* little girls.'

'Can he play games?'

'Surely. He can do any number of tricks. Would you like to see some?'

'Right away. I want Robbie to see him, too. —*Robbie!*' She

55

stopped, uncertainly, and frowned, 'I'll bet he's just staying in his room because he's mad at me for not taking him to the visivox. You'll have to explain to him, Daddy. He might not believe me, but he knows if you say it, it's so.'

Weston's lips grew tighter. He looked toward his wife but could not catch her eye.

Gloria turned precipitously and ran down the basement steps, shouting as she went, 'Robbie— Come and see what Daddy and Mamma brought me. They brought me a dog, Robbie.'

In a minute she had returned, a frightened little girl. 'Mamma, Robbie isn't in his room. Where is he?' There was no answer and George Weston coughed and was suddenly extremely interested in an aimlessly drifting cloud. Gloria's voice quavered on the verge of tears, 'Where's Robbie, Mamma?'

Mrs Weston sat down and drew her daughter gently to her, 'Don't feel bad, Gloria. Robbie has gone away, I think.'

'Gone *away*? Where? Where's he gone away, Mamma?'

'No one knows, darling. He just walked away. We've looked and we've looked and we've looked for him, but we can't find him.'

'You mean he'll never come back again?' Her eyes were round with horror.

'We may find him soon. We'll keep looking for him. And meanwhile you can play with your nice new doggie. Look at him! His name is Lightning and he can—'

But Gloria's eyelids had overflown, 'I don't want the nasty dog — I want Robbie. I want you to find me Robbie.' Her feelings became too deep for words, and she spluttered into a shrill wail.

Mrs Weston glanced at her husband for help, but he merely shuffled his feet morosely and did not withdraw his ardent stare from the heavens, so she bent to the task of consolation, 'Why do you cry, Gloria? Robbie was only a machine, just a nasty old machine. He wasn't alive at all.'

'He was *not* no machine!' screamed Gloria, fiercely and ungrammatically. 'He was a *person* just like you and me and he was my *friend*. I want him back. Oh, Mamma, I want him back.'

Her mother groaned in defeat and left Gloria to her sorrow.

'Let her have her cry out,' she told her husband. 'Childish griefs are never lasting. In a few days, she'll forget that awful robot ever existed.'

But time proved Mrs Weston a bit too optimistic. To be sure, Gloria ceased crying, but she ceased smiling, too, and the passing days found her ever more silent and shadowy. Gradually, her attitude of passive unhappiness wore Mrs Weston down and all that kept her from yielding was the impossibility of admitting defeat to her husband.

Then, one evening, she flounced into the living room, sat down, folded her arms and looked boiling mad.

Her husband stretched his neck in order to see her over his newspaper, 'What now, Grace?'

'It's that child, George. I've had to send back the dog today. Gloria positively couldn't stand the sight of him, she said. She's driving me into a nervous breakdown.'

Weston laid down the paper and a hopeful gleam entered his eye, 'Maybe— Maybe we ought to get Robbie back. It might be done, you know. I can get in touch with—'

'No!' she replied, grimly. 'I won't hear of it. We're not giving up that easily. My child shall *not* be brought up by a robot if it takes years to break her of it.'

Weston picked up his paper again with a disappointed air. 'A year of this will have me prematurely gray.'

'You're a big help, George,' was the frigid answer. 'What Gloria needs is a change of environment. Of course she can't forget Robbie here. How can she when every tree and rock reminds her of him? It is really the *silliest* situation I have ever heard of. Imagine a child pining away for the loss of a robot.'

'Well, stick to the point. What's the change in environment you're planning?'

'We're going to take her to New York.'

'The city! In August! Say, do you know what New York is like in August. It's unbearable.'

'Millions do bear it.'

'They don't have a place like this to go to. If they didn't have to stay in New York, they wouldn't.'

'Well, *we* have to. I say we're leaving now — or as soon as we can make the arrangements. In the city, Gloria will find sufficient interests and sufficient friends to perk her up and make her forget that machine.'

'Oh, Lord,' groaned the lesser half, 'those frying pavements!'

'We have to,' was the unshaken response. 'Gloria has lost five pounds in the last month and my little girl's health is more important to me than your comfort.'

'It's a pity you didn't think of your little girl's health before you deprived her of her pet robot,' he muttered — but to himself.

*   *   *

Gloria displayed immediate signs of improvement when told of the impending trip to the city. She spoke little of it, but when she did, it was always with lively anticipation. Again, she began to smile and to eat with something of her former appetite.

Mrs Weston hugged herself for joy and lost no opportunity to triumph over her still skeptical husband.

'You see, George, she helps with the packing like a little angel, and chatters away as if she hadn't a care in the world. It's just as I told you — all we need do is substitute other interests.'

'Hmpph,' was the skeptical response, 'I hope so.'

Preliminaries were gone through quickly. Arrangements were made for the preparation of their city home and a couple were engaged as housekeepers for the country home. When the day of the trip finally did come, Gloria was all but her old self again, and no mention of Robbie passed her lips at all.

In high good-humour the family took a taxi-gyro to the airport (Weston would have preferred using his own private 'gyro, but it was only a two-seater with no room for baggage) and entered the waiting liner.

'Come, Gloria,' called Mrs Weston. 'I've saved you a seat near the window so you can watch the scenery.'

Gloria trotted down the aisle cheerily, flattened her nose into a white oval against the thick clear glass, and watched with an intentness that increased as the sudden coughing of the motor drifted backward into the interior. She was too young to be frightened when the ground dropped away as if let through a trap-door and she herself suddenly became twice her usual weight, but not too young to be mightily interested. It wasn't until the ground had changed into a tiny patchwork quilt that she withdrew her nose, and faced her mother again.

'Will we soon be in the city, Mamma?' she asked, rubbing her chilled nose, and watching with interest as the patch of moisture which her breath had formed on the pane shrank slowly and vanished.

'In about half an hour, dear.' Then, with just the faintest trace of anxiety, 'Aren't you glad we're going? Don't you think you'll be very happy in the city with all the buildings and people and things to see. We'll go to the visivox every day and see shows and go to the circus and the beach and —'

'Yes, Mamma,' was Gloria's unenthusiastic rejoinder. The liner passed over a bank of clouds at the moment, and Gloria was instantly absorbed in the unusual spectacle of clouds underneath one. Then they were over clear sky again, and she turned to her mother with a sudden mysterious air of secret knowledge.

'I know why we're going to the city, Mamma.'

'Do you?' Mrs Weston was puzzled. 'Why, dear?'

'You didn't tell me because you wanted it to be a surprise, but I know.' For a moment, she was lost in admiration at her own acute penetration, and then she laughed gaily. 'We're going to New York so we can find Robbie, aren't we? — With detectives.'

The statement caught George Weston in the middle of a drink

of water, with disastrous results. There was a sort of strangled gasp, a geyser of water, and then a bout of choking coughs. When all was over, he stood there, a red-faced, water-drenched and very, very annoyed person.

Mrs Weston maintained her composure, but when Gloria repeated her question in a more anxious tone of voice, she found her temper rather bent.

'Maybe,' she retorted, tartly. 'Now sit and be still, for heaven's sake.'

*   *   *

New York City, AD 1998, was a paradise for the sightseer more than ever in its history. Gloria's parents realized this and made the most of it.

On direct orders from his wife, George Weston arranged to have his business take care of itself for a month or so, in order to be free to spend the time in what he termed 'dissipating Gloria to the verge of ruin.' Like everything else Weston did, this was gone about in an efficient, thorough, and businesslike way. Before the month had passed, nothing that could be done had not been done.

She was taken to the top of the half-mile tall Roosevelt Building, to gaze down in awe upon the jagged panorama of rooftops that blended far off in the fields of Long Island and the flatlands of New Jersey. They visited the zoos where Gloria stared in delicious fright at the 'real live lion' (rather disappointed that the keepers fed him raw steaks, instead of human beings, as she had expected), and asked insistently and peremptorily to see 'the whale'.

The various museums came in for their share of attention, together with the parks and the beaches and the aquarium.

She was taken halfway up the Hudson in an excursion steamer fitted out in the archaism of the mad Twenties. She travelled into the stratosphere on an exhibition trip, where the sky turned deep purple and the stars came out and the misty earth below looked like a huge concave bowl. Down under the waters of the Long Island Sound she was taken in a glass-walled sub-sea vessel, where in a green and wavering world, quaint and curious sea-things ogled her and wiggled suddenly away.

On a more prosaic level, Mrs Weston took her to the department stores where she could revel in another type of fairyland.

In fact, when the month had nearly sped, the Westons were convinced that everything conceivable had been done to take Gloria's mind once and for all off the departed Robbie — but they were not quite sure they had succeeded.

The fact remained that wherever Gloria went, she displayed the most absorbed and concentrated interest in such robots as happened to be present. No matter how exciting the spectacle before her, nor how novel to her girlish eyes, she turned away instantly if the corner of her eye caught a glimpse of metallic movement.

Mrs Weston went out of her way to keep Gloria away from all robots.

And the matter was finally climaxed in the episode at the Museum of Science and Industry. The Museum had announced a special 'Children's program' in which exhibits of scientific witchery scaled down to the child mind were to be shown. The Westons, of course, placed it upon their list of 'absolutely'.

It was while the Westons were standing totally absorbed in the exploits of a powerful electro-magnet that Mrs Weston suddenly became aware of the fact that Gloria was no longer with her. Initial panic gave away to calm decision and, enlisting the aid of three attendants, a careful search was begun.

Gloria, of course, was not one to wander aimlessly, however. For her age, she was an unusually determined and purposeful girl, quite full of the maternal genes in that respect. She had seen a huge sign on the third floor, which had said, 'This Way to the Talking Robot.' Having spelled it out to herself and having noticed that her parents did not seem to wish to move in the

61

proper direction, she did the obvious thing. Waiting for an opportune moment of parental distraction, she calmly disengaged herself and followed the sign.

*   *   *

The Talking Robot was a *tour de force,* a thoroughly impractical device, possessing publicity value only. Once an hour, an escorted group stood before it and asked questions of the robot engineer in charge in careful whispers. Those the engineer decided were suitable for the robot's circuits were transmitted to the Talking Robot.

It was rather dull. It may be nice to know that the square of fourteen is one hundred ninety-six, that the temperature at the moment is 72 degrees Fahrenheit, and the air-pressure 30.02 inches of mercury, that the atomic weight of sodium is 23, but one doesn't really need a robot for that. One especially does not need an unwieldly, totally immobile mass of wires and coils spreading over twenty-five square yards.

Few people bothered to return for a second helping, but one girl in her middle teens sat quietly on a bench waiting for a third. She was the only one in the room when Gloria entered.

Gloria did not look at her. To her at the moment, another human being was but an inconsiderable item. She saved her attention for this large thing with the wheels. For a moment, she hesitated in dismay. It didn't look like any robot she had ever seen.

Cautiously and doubtfully she raised her treble voice, 'Please, Mr Robot, sir, are you the Talking Robot, sir?' She wasn't sure, but it seemed to her that a robot that actually talked was worth a great deal of politeness.

(The girl in her mid teens allowed a look of intense concentration to cross her thin, plain face. She whipped out a small notebook and began writing in rapid pot-hooks.)

There was an oily whir of gears and a mechanically-timbred voice boomed out in words that lacked accent and intonation, 'I

— am — the — robot — that — talks.'

Gloria stared at it ruefully. It *did* talk, but the sound came from inside somewheres. There was no *face* to talk to. She said, 'Can you help me, Mr Robot, sir?'

The Talking Robot was designed to answer questions, and only such questions as it could answer had ever been put to it. It was quite confident of its ability, therefore, 'I — can — help — you.'

'Thank you, Mr Robot, sir. Have you seen Robbie?'

'Who — is Robbie?'

'He's a robot, Mr Robot, sir.' She stretched to tip-toes. 'He's about so high, Mr Robot, sir, only higher, and he's very nice. He's got a head, you know. I mean you haven't, but he has, Mr Robot, sir.'

The Talking Robot had been left behind, 'A — robot?'

'Yes, Mr Robot, sir. A robot just like you, except he can't talk, of course, and — looks like a real person.'

'A — robot — like — me?'

'Yes, Mr Robot, sir.'

To which the Talking Robot's only response was an erratic splutter and an occasional incoherent sound. The radical generalization offered it, i.e. its existence, not as a particular object, but as a member of a general group, was too much for it. Loyally, it tried to encompass the concept and half a dozen coils burnt out. Little warning signals were buzzing.

(The girl in her mid-teens left at that point. She had enough for her Physics 1 paper on 'Practical Aspects of Robotics.' This paper was Susan Calvin's first of many on the subject.)

Gloria stood waiting, with carefully concealed impatience, for the machine's answer when she heard the cry behind her of 'There she is,' and recognized that cry as her mother's.

'What are you doing here, you bad girl?' cried Mrs Weston, anxiety dissolving at once into anger. 'Do you know you frightened your mamma and daddy almost to death? Why did you run away?'

The robot engineer had also dashed in, tearing his hair, and

63

demanding who of the gathering crowd had tampered with the machine. 'Can't anybody read signs?' he yelled. 'You're not allowed in here without an attendant.'

Gloria raised her grieved voice over the din, 'I only came to see the Talking Robot, Mamma, I thought he might know where Robbie was because they're both robots.' And then, as the thought of Robbie was suddenly brought forcefully home to her, she burst into a sudden storm of tears, 'And I *got* to find Robbie, Mamma. I *got* to.'

Mrs Weston strangled a cry, and said, 'Oh, good Heavens. Come home, George. This is more than I can stand.'

That evening, George Weston left for several hours, and the next morning, he approached his wife with something that looked suspiciously like smug complacence.

'I've got an idea, Grace.'

'About what?' was the gloomy, uninterested query.

'About Gloria.'

'You're not going to suggest buying back that robot?'

'No, of course not.'

'Then go ahead. I might as well listen to you. Nothing *I've* done seems to have done any good.'

'All right. Here's what I've been thinking. The whole trouble with Gloria is that she thinks of Robbie as a *person* and not as a *machine*. Naturally, she can't forget him. Now if we managed to convince her that Robbie was nothing more than a mess of steel and copper in the form of sheets and wires with electricity its juice of life, how long would her longings last. It's the psychological attack, if you see my point.'

'How do you plan to do it?'

'Simple. Where do you suppose I went last night? I persuaded Robertson of US Robots and Mechanical Men, Inc to arrange for a complete tour of his premises tomorrow. The three of us will go, and by the time we're through, Gloria will have it drilled into her that a robot is *not* alive.'

Mrs Weston's eyes widened gradually and something glinted

in her eyes that was quite like sudden admiration, 'Why, George, that's a *good* idea.'

And George Weston's vest buttons strained. 'Only kind I have,' he said.

*   *   *

Mr Struthers was a conscientious General Manager and naturally inclined to be a bit talkative. The combination, therefore, resulted in a tour that was fully explained, perhaps even over-abundantly explained, at every step. However, Mrs Weston was not bored. Indeed, she stopped him several times and begged him to repeat his statements in simpler language so that Gloria might understand. Under the influence of this appreciation of his narrative powers, Mr Struthers expanded genially and became ever more communicative, if possible.

George Weston, himself, showed a gathering impatience.

'Pardon me, Struthers,' he said, breaking into the middle of a lecture on the photo-electric cell, 'haven't you a section of the factory where only robot labour is employed?'

'Eh? Oh, yes! Yes, indeed!' He smiled at Mrs Weston. 'A vicious circle in a way, robots creating more robots. Of course, we are not making a general practice out of it. For one thing, the unions would never let us. But we can turn out a very few robots using robot labour exclusively, merely as a sort of scientific experiment. You see,' he tapped his pince-nez into one palm argumentatively, 'what the labour unions don't realize — and I say this as a man who has always been very sympathetic with the labour movement in general — is that the advent of the robot, while involving some dislocation to begin with, will inevitably —'

'Yes, Struthers,' said Weston, 'but about that section of the factory you speak of — may we see it? It would be very interesting, I'm sure.'

'Yes! Yes, of course!' Mr Struthers replaced his pince-nez in one conclusive movement and gave vent to a soft cough of discomfiture. 'Follow me, please.'

He was comparatively quiet while leading the three through a long corridor and down a flight of stairs. Then, when they had entered a large well-lit room that buzzed with metallic activity, the sluices opened and the flood of explanation poured forth again.

'There you are!' he said with pride in his voice. 'Robots only! Five men act as overseers and they don't even stay in this room. In five years, that is, since we began this project, not a single accident has occurred. Of course, the robots here assembled are comparatively simple, but . . .'

The General Manager's voice had long died to a rather soothing murmur in Gloria's ears. The whole trip seemed rather dull and pointless to her, though there *were* many robots in sight. None were even remotely like Robbie, though, and she surveyed them with open contempt.

In this room, there weren't any people at all, she noticed. Then her eyes fell upon six or seven robots busily engaged at a round table half-way across the room. They widened in incredulous surprise. It was a big room. She couldn't see for sure, but one of the robots looked like — looked like — *it was!*

'Robbie!' Her shriek pierced the air, and one of the robots about the table faltered and dropped the tool he was holding. Gloria went almost mad with joy. Squeezing through the railing before either parent could stop her, she dropped lightly to the floor a few feet below, and ran toward her Robbie, arms waving and hair flying.

And the three horrified adults, as they stood frozen in their tracks, saw what the excited little girl did not see, — a huge, lumbering tractor bearing blindly down upon its appointed track.

It took split-seconds for Weston to come to his senses, and those split-seconds meant everything, for Gloria could not be overtaken. Although Weston vaulted the railing in a wild attempt, it was obviously hopeless. Mr Struthers signalled wildly to the overseers to stop the tractor, but the overseers were only human and it took time to act.

It was only Robbie that acted immediately and with precision. With metal legs eating up the space between himself and his little mistress he charged down from the opposite direction. Everything then happened at once. With one sweep of an arm, Robbie snatched up Gloria, slackening his speed not one iota, and, consequently, knocking every breath of air out of her. Weston, not quite comprehending all that was happening, felt, rather than saw, Robbie brush past him, and came to a sudden bewildered halt. The tractor intersected Gloria's path half a second after Robbie had, rolled on ten feet further and came to a grinding, long-drawn-out stop.

Gloria regained her breath, submitted to a series of passionate hugs on the part of both her parents and turned eagerly toward Robbie. As far as she was concerned, nothing had happened except that she had found her friend.

But Mrs Weston's expression had changed from one of relief to one of dark suspicion. She turned to her husband, and, despite her disheveled and undignified appearance, managed to look quite formidable, '*You* engineered this, *didn't* you?'

George Weston swabbed at a hot forehead with his handkerchief. His hand was unsteady, and his lips could curve only into a tremulous and exceedingly weak smile.

Mrs Weston pursued the thought, 'Robbie wasn't designed for engineering or construction work. He couldn't be of any use to them. You had him placed there deliberately so that Gloria would find him. You know you did.'

'Well, I did,' said Weston. 'But, Grace, how was I to know the reunion would be so violent? And Robbie has saved her life; you'll have to admit that. You *can't* send him away again.'

Grace Weston considered. She turned toward Gloria and Robbie and watched them abstractedly for a moment. Gloria had a grip about the robot's neck and would have asphyxiated any creature but one of metal, and was prattling nonsense in half-hysterical frenzy. Robbie's chrome-steel arms (capable of bending a bar of steel two inches in diameter into a pretzel)

67

wound about the little girl gently and lovingly, and his eyes glowed a deep, deep red.

'Well,' said Mrs Weston, at last, 'I guess he can stay with us until he rusts.'

Grandpa

JAMES H. SCHMITZ

*Born 1911. American. He published his first science
fiction story in 1942 and now has numerous
books and over eighty stories in print.*

A green-winged downy thing as big as a hen fluttered along the
hillside to a point directly above Cord's head and hovered there,
twenty feet above him. Cord, a fifteen-year-old human being,
leaned back against a skipboat parked on the equator of a world
that had known human beings for only the past four Earth-years,
and eyed the thing speculatively. The thing was, in the free and
easy terminology of the Sutang Colonial Team, a swamp bug.
Concealed in the downy fur behind the bug's head was a second,
smaller, semi-parasitical thing, classed as a bug rider.

The bug itself looked like a new species to Cord. Its parasite
might or might not turn out to be another unknown. Cord was a
natural research man; his first glimpse of the odd flying team had
sent endless curiosities thrilling through him. How did that
particular phenomenon tick, and *why*? What fascinating things,
once you'd learned about it, could you get it to *do*?

Normally, he was hampered by circumstances in carrying out
any such investigation. Junior colonial students like Cord were
expected to confine their curiosity to the pattern of research set
up by the Station to which they were attached. Cord's inclination
towards independent experiments had got him into disfavour with
his immediate superiors before this.

He sent a casual glance in the direction of the Yoger Bay
Colonial Station behind him. No signs of human activity about that
low, fortresslike bulk in the hill. Its central lock was still closed. In
fifteen minutes, it was scheduled to be opened to let out the
Planetary Regent, who was inspecting the Yoger Bay Station and

its principal activities today.

Fifteen minutes was time enough to find out something about the new bug, Cord decided.

But he'd have to collect it first.

*   *   *

He slid out one of the two handguns holstered at his side. This one was his own property: a Vanadian projectile weapon. Cord thumbed it to position for anaesthetic small-game missiles and brought the hovering swamp bug down, drilled neatly and microscopically through the head.

As the bug hit the ground, the rider left its back. A tiny scarlet demon, round and bouncy as a rubber ball, it shot towards Cord in three long hops, mouth wide to sink home inch-long, venom-dripping fangs. Rather breathlessly, Cord triggered the gun again and knocked it out in mid-leap. A new species, all right! Most bug riders were harmless plant eaters, mere suckers of vegetable juice —

'Cord!' A feminine voice.

Cord swore softly. He hadn't heard the central lock click open. She must have come around from the other side of the station.

'Hello, Grayan!' he shouted innocently without looking round. 'Come and see what I've got! New species!'

Grayan Mahoney, a slender, black-haired girl two years older than himself, came trotting down the hillside towards him. She was Sutang's star colonial student, and the station manager, Nirmond, indicated from time to time that she was a fine example for Cord to pattern his own behaviour on. In spite of that, she and Cord were good friends.

'Cord, you idiot,' she scowled as she came up. 'Stop playing the collector! If the Regent came out now, you'd be sunk. Nirmond's been telling her about you!'

'Telling her what?' Cord asked, startled.

'For one thing,' Grayan reported, 'that you don't keep up on your assigned work.'

70

'Golly!' gulped Cord, dismayed.

'Golly, is right! I keep warning you!'

'What'll I do?'

'Start acting as if you had good sense mainly.' Grayan grinned suddenly. 'But if you mess up our tour of the Bay Farms today, you'll be off the Team for good!'

She turned to go. 'You might as well put the skipboat back; we're not using it. Nirmond's driving us down to the edge of the bay in a treadcar, and we'll take a raft from there.'

Leaving his newly bagged specimens to revive by themselves and flutter off again, Cord hurriedly flew the skipboat around the station and rolled it back into its stall.

$$* \qquad * \qquad *$$

Three rafts lay moored just offshore in the marshy cove at the edge of which Nirmond had stopped the treadcar. They looked somewhat like exceptionally broad-brimmed, well-worn sugar-loaf hats floating out there, green and leathery. Or like lily pads twenty-five feet across, with the upper section of a big, grey-green pineapple growing from the centre of each. Plant animals of some sort. Sutang was too new to have had its phyla sorted out into anything remotely like an orderly classification. The rafts were a local oddity which had been investigated and could be regarded as harmless and moderately useful. Their usefulness lay in the fact that they were employed as a rather slow means of transportation about the shallow, swampy waters of the Yoger Bay. That was as far as the Team's interest in them went at present.

The Regent stood up from the back seat of the car, where she was sitting next to Cord. There were only four in the party; Grayan was up front with Nirmond.

'Are those our vehicles?' The Regent sounded amused.

Nirmond grinned. 'Don't underestimate them, Dane! They could become an important economic factor in this region in time. But, as a matter of fact, these three are smaller than I like to

71

use.' He was peering about the reedy edges of the cove. 'There's a regular monster parked here usually —'

Grayan turned to Cord. 'Maybe Cord knows where Grandpa is hiding.'

It was well-meant, but Cord had been hoping nobody would ask him about Grandpa. Now they all looked at him.

'Oh, you want Grandpa?' he said, somewhat flustered. 'Well I left him . . . I mean I saw him a couple of weeks ago about a mile south from here —'

Nirmond grunted and told the Regent, 'The rafts tend to stay wherever they're left, providing it's shallow and muddy. They use a hair-root system to draw chemicals and microscopic nourishment directly from the bottom of the bay. Well — Grayan, would you like to drive us there?'

Cord settled back unhappily as the treadcar lurched into motion. Nirmond suspected he'd used Grandpa for one of his unauthorized tours of the area, and Nirmond was quite right.

'I understand you're an expert with these rafts, Cord,' Dane said from beside him. 'Grayan told me we couldn't find a better steersman, or pilot, or whatever you call it, for our trip today.'

'I can handle them,' Cord said, perspiring. 'They don't give you any trouble!' He didn't feel he'd made a good impression on the Regent so far. Dane was a young, handsome-looking woman with an easy way of talking and laughing, but she wasn't the head of the Sutang Colonial Team for nothing.

'There's one big advantage our beasties have over a skip-boat too,' Nirmond remarked from the front seat. 'You don't have to worry about a snapper trying to climb on board with you!' He went on to describe the stinging ribbon-tentacles the rafts spread around them under the water to discourage creatures that might make a meal off their tender underparts. The snappers and two or three other active and aggressive species of the bay hadn't yet learned it was foolish to attack armed human beings in a boat, but they would skitter hurriedly out of the path of a leisurely perambulating raft.

72

Cord was happy to be ignored for the moment. The Regent, Nirmond, and Grayan were all Earth people, which was true of most of the members of the Team; and Earth people made him uncomfortable, particularly in groups. Vanadia, his own home world, had barely graduated from the status of Earth colony itself, which might explain the difference.

The treadcar swung around and stopped, and Grayan stood up in the front seat, pointing. 'That's Grandpa, over there!'

Dane also stood up and whistled softly, apparently impressed by Grandpa's fifty-foot spread. Cord looked around in surprise. He was pretty sure this was several hundred yards from the spot where he'd left the big raft two weeks ago; and, as Nirmond said, they didn't usually move about by themselves.

Puzzled, he followed the others down a narrow path to the water, hemmed in by tree-sized reeds. Now and then he got a glimpse of Grandpa's swimming platform, the rim of which just touched the shore. Then the path opened out, and he saw the whole raft lying in sunlit, shallow water; and he stopped short, startled.

Nirmond was about to step up on the platform, ahead of Dane.

'Wait!' Cord shouted. His voice sounded squeaky with alarm. 'Stop!'

He came running forward.

'What's the matter, Cord?' Nirmond's voice was quiet and urgent.

'Don't get on that raft — it's changed!' Cord's voice sounded wobbly, even to himself. 'Maybe it's not even Grandpa —'

He saw he was wrong on the last point before he'd finished the sentence. Scattered along the rim of the raft were discoloured spots left by a variety of heat-guns, one of which had been his own. It was the way you goaded the sluggish and mindless things into motion. Cord pointed at the cone-shaped central projection. 'There — his head! He's sprouting!'

Grandpa's head, as befitted his girth, was almost twelve feet high and equally wide. It was armour-plated like the back of a

73

saurian to keep off plant suckers, but two weeks ago it had been an otherwise featureless knob, like those on all other rafts. Now scores of long, kinky, leafless vines had grown out from all surfaces of the cone, like green wires. Some were drawn up like tightly coiled springs, others trailed limply to the platform and over it. The top of the cone was dotted with angry red buds, rather like pimples, which hadn't been there before either. Grandpa looked unhealthy.

'Well,' Nirmond said, 'so it is. Sprouting!' Grayan made a choked sound. Nirmond glanced at Cord as if puzzled. 'Is that all that was bothering you, Cord?'

'Well, sure!' Cord began excitedly. He had caught the significance of the word 'all'; his hackles were still up, and he was shaking. 'None of them ever —'

Then he stopped. He could tell by their faces, that they hadn't got it. Or rather, that they'd got it all right but simply weren't going to let it change their plans. The rafts were classified as harmless, according to the Regulations. Until proved otherwise, they would continue to be regarded as harmless. You didn't waste time quibbling with the Regulations — even if you were the Planetary Regent. You didn't feel you had the time to waste.

He tried again. 'Look —' he began. What he wanted to tell them was that Grandpa with one unknown factor added wasn't Grandpa any more. He was an unpredictable, oversized life form, to be investigated with cautious thoroughness till you knew what the unknown factor meant. He stared at them helplessly.

Dane turned to Nirmond. 'Perhaps you'd better check,' she said. She didn't add, '—to reassure the boy!' but that was what she meant.

Cord felt himself flushing. But there was nothing he could say or do now except watch Nirmond walk steadily across the platform. Grandpa shivered slightly a few times, but the rafts always did that when someone first stepped on them. The station manager stopped before one of the kinky sprouts, touched it, and then gave it a tug. He reached up and poked at the lowest of the

74

budlike growths. 'Odd-looking things!' he called back. He gave Cord another glance. 'Well, everything seems harmless enough, Cord. Coming aboard, everyone?'

It was like dreaming a dream in which you yelled and yelled at people and couldn't make them hear you! Cord stepped up stiff-legged on the platform behind Dane and Grayan. He knew exactly what would have happened if he'd hesitated even a moment. One of them would have said in a friendly voice, careful not to let it sound contemptuous: 'You don't have to come along if you don't want to, Cord!'

Grayan had unholstered her heat-gun and was ready to start Grandpa moving out into the channels of the Yoger Bay.

Cord hauled out his own heat-gun and said roughly, 'I was to do that!'

'All right, Cord.' She gave him a brief, impersonal smile and stood aside.

They were so infuriatingly polite!

For a while, Cord almost hoped that something insecure and catastrophic would happen promptly to teach the Team people a lesson. But nothing did. As always, Grandpa shook himself vaguely and experimentally when he felt the heat on one edge of the platform and then decided to withdraw from it, all of which was standard procedure. Under the water, out of sight, were the raft's working sections: short, thick leaf-structures shaped like paddles and designed to work as such, along with the slimy nettle-streamers which kept the vegetarians of the Yoger Bay away, and a jungle of hair roots through which Grandpa sucked nourishment from the mud and the sluggish waters of the bay and with which he also anchored himself.

The paddles started churning, the platform quivered, the hair roots were hauled out of the mud; and Grandpa was on his ponderous way.

Cord switched off the heat, reholstered his gun, and stood up. Once in motion, the rafts tended to keep travelling unhurriedly for quite a while. To stop them, you gave them a touch of heat

75

along their leading edge; and they could be turned in any direction by using the gun lightly on the opposite side of the platform. It was simple enough.

Cord didn't look at the others. He was still burning inside. He watched the reed beds move past and open out, giving him glimpses of the misty, yellow and green and blue expanses of the brackish bay ahead. Behind the mist, to the west, were the Yoger Straits, tricky and ugly water when the tides were running; and beyond the Straits lay the open sea, the great Zlanti Deep, which was another world entirely and one of which he hadn't seen much as yet.

Grayan called from beside Dane, 'What's the best route from here into the farms, Cord?'

'The big channel to the right,' he answered. He added somewhat sullenly, 'We're headed for it!'

Grayan came over to him. 'The Regent doesn't want to see all of it' she said, lowering her voice. 'The algae and plankton beds first. Then as much of the mutated grains as we can show her in about three hours. Steer for the ones that have been doing best, and you'll keep Nirmond happy!'

She gave him a conspiratorial wink. Cord looked after her uncertainly. You couldn't tell from her behaviour that anything was wrong. Maybe —

He had a flare of hope. It was hard not to like the Team people, even when they were being rock-headed about their Regulations. Anyway, the day wasn't over yet. He might still redeem himself in the Regent's opinion.

Cord had a sudden cheerful, if improbable vision of some bay monster plunging up on the raft with snapping jaws; and of himself alertly blowing out what passed for the monster's brains before anyone else — Nirmond in particular — was even aware of the threat. The bay monsters shunned Grandpa, of course, but there might be ways of tempting one of them.

So far, Cord realized, he'd been letting his feelings control him. It was time to start thinking!

76

Grandpa first. So he'd sprouted — green vines and red buds, purpose unknown, but with no change observable in his behaviour-patterns otherwise. He was the biggest raft in this end of the bay, though all of them had been growing steadily in the two years since Cord had first seen one. Sutang's seasons changed slowly; its year was somewhat more than five Earth-years long. The first Team members to land here hadn't yet seen a full year pass.

Grandpa then was showing a seasonal change. The other rafts, not quite so far developed, would be reacting similarly a little later. Plant animals — they might be blossoming, preparing to propagate.

'Grayan,' he called, 'how do the rafts get started? When they're small, I mean.'

'Nobody knows yet,' she said. 'We were just talking about it. About half of the coastal marsh-fauna of the continent seems to go through a preliminary larval stage in the sea.' She nodded at the red buds on the raft's cone. 'It *looks* as if Grandpa is going to produce flowers and let the wind or tide take the seeds out through the Straits.'

It made sense. It also knocked out Cord's still half-held hope that the change in Grandpa might turn out to be drastic enough, in some way, to justify his reluctance to get on board. Cord studied Grandpa's armoured head carefully once more — unwilling to give up that hope entirely. There were a series of vertical gummy black slits between the armour plates, which hadn't been in evidence two weeks ago either. It looked as if Grandpa was beginning to come apart at the seams. Which might indicate that the rafts, big as they grew to be, didn't outlive a full seasonal cycle, but came to flower at about this time of Sutang's year, and died. However, it was a safe bet that Grandpa wasn't going to collapse into senile decay before they completed their trip today.

Cord gave up on Grandpa. The other notion returned to him — perhaps he *could* coax an obliging bay monster into action that

77

would show the Regent he was no sissy!

Because the monsters were there all right.

Kneeling at the edge of the platform and peering down into the wine-coloured, clear water of the deep channel they were moving through, Cord could see a fair selection of them at almost any moment.

Some five or six snappers, for one thing. Like big, flattened crayfish, chocolate-brown mostly, with green and red spots on their carapaced backs. In some areas they were so thick you'd wonder what they found to live on, except that they ate almost anything, down to chewing up the mud in which they squatted. However, they preferred their food in large chunks and alive, which was one reason you didn't go swimming in the bay. They would attack a boat on occasion; but the excited manner in which the ones he saw were scuttling off towards the edges of the channel showed they wanted nothing to do with a big moving raft.

Dotted across the bottom were two-foot round holes which looked vacant at the moment. Normally, Cord knew, there would be a head filling each of those holes. The heads consisted mainly of triple sets of jaws, held open patiently like so many traps to grab at anything that came within range of the long wormlike bodies behind the heads. But Grandpa's passage, waving his stingers like transparent pennants through the water, had scared the worms out of sight, too.

Otherwise, mostly schools of small stuff — and then a flash of wicked scarlet, off to the left behind the raft, darting out from the reeds, turning its needle-nose into their wake.

Cord watched it without moving. He knew that creature, though it was rare in the bay and hadn't been classified. Swift, vicious — alert enough to snap swamp bugs out of the air as they fluttered across the surface. And he'd tantalized one with fishing tackle once into leaping up on a moored raft, where it had flung itself about furiously until he was able to shoot it.

'What fantastic creatures!' Dane's voice just behind him.

'Yellowheads,' said Nirmond. 'They've got a high utility rating.'

Keep down the bugs.'

Cord stood up casually. It was no time for tricks! The reed bed to their right was thick with Yellowheads, a colony of them. Vaguely froggy things, man sized and better. Of all the creatures he'd discovered in the bay, Cord like them least. The flabby, sack-like bodies clung with four thin limbs to the upper section of the twenty-foot reeds that lined the channel. They hardly ever moved, but their huge bulging eyes seemed to take in everything that went on about them. Every so often, a downy swamp bug came close enough; and a Yellowhead would open its vertical, enormous tooth-lined slash of a mouth, extend the whole front of its face like a bellows in a flashing strike; and the bug would be gone. They might be useful, but Cord hated them.

'Ten years from now we should know what the cycle of coastal life is like,' Nirmond said. 'When we set up the Yoger Bay Station there were no Yellowheads here. They came the following year. Still with traces of the oceanic larval form; but the metamorphosis was almost complete. About twelve inches long —'

Dane remarked that the same pattern was duplicated endlessly elsewhere. The Regent was inspecting the Yellowhead colony with field glasses; she put them down now, looked at Cord, and smiled, 'How far to the farms?'

'About twenty minutes.'

'The key', Nirmond said, 'seems to be the Zlanti Basin. It must be almost a soup of life in spring.'

'It is,' nodded Dane, who had been here in Sutang's spring, four Earth-years ago. 'It's beginning to look as if the Basin alone might justify colonization. The question is still' — she gestured towards the Yellowheads — 'how do creatures like that get here?'

*   *   *

They walked off towards the other side of the raft, arguing about ocean currents. Cord might have followed. But something splashed back of them, off to the left and not too far back. He

79

stayed, watching.

After a moment, he saw the big Yellowhead. It had slipped down from its reedy perch, which was what had caused the splash. Almost submerged at the water line, it stared after the raft with huge, pale-green eyes. To Cord, it seemed to look directly at him. In that moment, he knew for the first time why he didn't like Yellowheads. There was something very like intelligence in that look, an alien calculation. In creatures like that, intelligence seemed out of place. What use could they have for it?

A little shiver went over him when it sank completely under the water and he realized it intended to swim after the raft. But it was mostly excitement. He had never seen a Yellowhead come down out of the reeds before. The obliging monster he'd been looking for might be presenting itself in an unexpected way.

Half a minute later, he watched it again, swimming awkwardly far down. It had no immediate intention of boarding, at any rate. Cord saw it come into the area of the raft's trailing stingers. It manoeuvred its way between them, with curiously human swimming motions, and went out of sight under the platform.

He stood up, wondering what it meant. The Yellowhead had appeared to know about the stingers; there had been an air of purpose in every move of its approach. He was tempted to tell the others about it, but there was the moment of triumph he could have if it suddenly came slobbering up over the edge of the platform and he nailed it before their eyes.

It was almost time anyway to turn the raft in towards the farms. If nothing happened before then —

He watched. Almost five minutes, but no sign of the Yellowhead. Still wondering, a little uneasy, he gave Grandpa a calculated needling of heat.

After a moment, he repeated it. Then he drew a deep breath and forgot all about the Yellowhead.

'Nirmond!' he called sharply.

The three of them were standing near the centre of the platform, next to the big armoured cone, looking ahead at the farms. They glanced around.

'What's the matter now, Cord?'

Cord couldn't say it for a moment. He was suddenly, terribly scared again. Something *had* gone wrong!

'The raft won't turn!' he told them.

'Give it a real burn this time!' Nirmond said.

Cord glanced up at him. Nirmond, standing a few steps in front of Dane and Grayan as if he wanted to protect them, had begun to look a little strained, and no wonder. Cord already had pressed the gun to three different points on the platform; but Grandpa appeared to have developed a sudden anaesthesia for heat. They kept moving out steadily towards the centre of the bay.

Now Cord held his breath, switched the heat on full, and let Grandpa have it. A six-inch patch on the platform blistered up instantly, turned brown, then black —

Grandpa stopped dead. Just like that.

'That's right! Keep burn —' Nirmond didn't finish his order.

A giant shudder. Cord staggered back towards the water. Then the whole edge of the raft came curling up behind him and went down again smacking the bay with a sound like a cannon shot. He flew forward off his feet, hit the platform face down, and flattened himself against it. It swelled up beneath him. Two more enormous slaps and joltings. Then quiet. He looked round for the others.

He lay within twelve feet of the central cone. Some twenty or thirty of the mysterious new vines the cone had sprouted were stretched stiffly towards him now, like so many thin green fingers. They couldn't quite reach him. The nearest tip was still ten inches from his shoes.

But Grandpa had caught the others, all three of them. They were tumbled together at the foot of the cone, wrapped in a stiff network of green vegetable ropes, and they didn't move.

Cord drew his feet up cautiously, prepared for another earthquake reaction. But nothing happened. Then he discovered that Grandpa was back in motion on his previous course. The heat-gun had vanished. Gently, he took out the Vanadian gun.

A voice, thin and pain-filled, spoke to him from one of the three huddled bodies.

'Cord? It didn't get you?' It was the Regent.

'No,' he said, keeping his voice low. He realized suddenly he'd simply assumed they were all dead. Now he felt sick and shaky.

'What are you doing?'

Cord looked at Grandpa's big, armour-plated head with a certain hunger. The cones were hollowed out inside, the station's lab had decided their chief function was to keep enough air trapped under the rafts to float them. But in that central section was also the organ that controlled Grandpa's overall reactions.

He said softly. 'I have a gun and twelve heavy-duty explosive bullets. Two of them will blow that cone apart.'

'No good, Cord!' the pain-racked voice told him: 'If the thing sinks, we'll die anyway. You have anaesthetic charges for that gun of yours?'

He stared at her back. 'Yes.'

'Give Nirmond and the girl a shot each, before you do anything else. Directly into the spine, if you can. But don't come any closer—'

Somehow, Cord couldn't argue with that voice. He stood up up carefully. The gun made two soft spitting sounds.

'All right,' he said hoarsely. 'What do I do now?'

Dane was silent a moment. 'I'm sorry, Cord, I can't tell you that. I'll tell you what I can—'

She paused for some seconds again.

'This thing didn't try to kill us, Cord. It could have easily. It's incredibly strong. I saw it break Nirmond's legs. But as soon as we stopped moving, it just held us. They were both unconscious then–

'You've got that to go on. It was trying to pitch you within reach of its vines or tendrils, or whatever they are, too, wasn't it?'

'I think so,' Cord said shakily. That was what had happened, of course; and at any moment Grandpa might try again.

'Now it's feeding us some sort of anaesthetic of its own through those vines. Tiny thorns. A sort of numbness —' Dane's voice trailed off a moment. Then she said clearly, 'Look, Cord — it seems we're food it's storing up! You get that?'

'Yes,' he said.

'Seeding time for the rafts. There are analogues. Live food for its seed probably; not for the raft. One couldn't have counted on that. Cord?'

'Yes, I'm here.'

'I want,' said Dane, 'to stay awake as long as I can. But there's really just one other thing — this raft's going somewhere, to some particularly favourable location. And that might be very near shore. You might make it in then; otherwise it's up to you. But keep your head and wait for a chance. No heroics, understand?'

'Sure, I understand,' Cord told her. He realised then that he was talking reassuringly, as if it wasn't the Planetary Regent but someone like Grayan.

'Nirmond's the worst,' Dane said. 'The girl was knocked unconscious at once. If it weren't for my arm — but, if we can get help in five hours or so, everything should be all right. Let me know if anything happens, Cord.'

'I will,' Cord said gently again. Then he sighted his gun carefully at a point between Dane's shoulder-blades, and the anaesthetic chamber made its soft, spitting sound once more. Dane's taut body relaxed slowly, and that was all.

There was no point Cord could see in letting her stay awake; because they weren't going anywhere near shore. The reed beds and the channels were already behind them, and Grandpa hadn't changed direction by the fraction of a degree. He was moving out into the open bay — and he was picking up company!

So far, Cord could count seven big rafts within two miles of them; and on the three that were closest he could make out a sprouting of new green vines. All of them were travelling in a straight direction; and the common point they were all headed for appeared to be the roaring centre of the Yoger Straits, now some three miles away!

Behind the Straits, the cold Zlanti Deep — the rolling fogs, and

83

the open sea! It might be seeding time for the rafts, but it looked as if they weren't going to distribute their seeds in the bay . . .

Cord was a fine swimmer. He had a gun and he had a knife; in spite of what Dane had said, he might have stood a chance among the killers of the bay. But it would be a very small chance, at best. And it wasn't, he thought, as if there weren't still other possibilities. He was going to keep his head.

Except by accident, of course, nobody was going to come looking for them in time to do any good. If anyone did look, it would be around the Bay Farms. There were a number of rafts moored there; and it would be assumed they'd used one of them. Now and then something unexpected happened and somebody simply vanished; by the time it was figured out just what had happened on this occasion, it would be much too late.

Neither was anybody likely to notice within the next few hours that the rafts had started migrating out of the swamps through the Yoger Straits. There was a small weather station a little inland, on the north side of the Straits, which used a helicopter occasionally. It was about as improbable, Cord decided dismally, that they'd use it in the right spot just now as it would be for a jet transport to happen to come in low enough to spot them.

The fact that it was up to him, as the Regent had said, sank in a little more after that!

Simply because he was going to try it sooner or later, he carried out an experiment next that he knew couldn't work. He opened the gun's anaesthetic chamber and counted out fifty pellets — rather hurriedly because he didn't particularly want to think of what he might be using them for eventually. There were around three hundred charges left in the chamber then; and in the next few minutes Cord carefully planted a third of them in Grandpa's head.

He stopped after that. A whale might have showed signs of somnolence under a lesser load. Grandpa paddled on undisturbed. Perhaps he had become a little numb in spots, but his cells weren't equipped to distribute the soporific effect of that type of drug.

There wasn't anything else Cord could think of doing before they reached the Straits. At the rate they were moving, he calculated that would happen in something less than an hour; and if they did pass through the Straits, he was going to risk a swim. He didn't think Dane would have disapproved, under the circumstances. If the raft simply carried them all out into the foggy vastness of the Zlanti Deep, there would be no practical chance of survival left at all.

Meanwhile, Grandpa was definitely picking up speed. And there were other changes going on — minor ones, but still a little awe-inspiring to Cord. The pimply-looking red buds that dotted the upper part of the cone were opening out gradually. From the centre of most of them protruded something like a thin, wet, scarlet worm: a worm that twisted weakly, extended itself by an inch or so, rested, and twisted again, and stretched up a little farther, groping into the air. The vertical black slits between the armour plates looked deeper and wider than they had been even some minutes ago; a dark, thick liquid dripped slowly from several of them.

In other circumstances Cord knew he would have been fascinated by these developments in Grandpa. As it was, they drew his suspicious attention only because he didn't know what they meant.

Then something quite horrible happened suddenly. Grayan started moaning loudly and terribly and twisted almost completely around. Afterwards, Cord knew it hadn't been a second before he stopped her struggles and the sounds together with another anaesthetic pellet; but the vines had tightened their grip on her first, not flexibly but like the digging, bony, green talons of some monstrous bird of prey.

*   *   *

White and sweating, Cord put his gun down slowly while the vines relaxed again. Grayan didn't seem to have suffered any additional harm; and she would certainly have been the first to point out that his murderous rage might have been as intelligently directed against a machine. But for some moments Cord continued to luxuriate furiously in the thought that, at any instant he chose, he could still turn the raft very quickly into a ripped and exploded mess of sinking vegetation.

Instead, and more sensibly, he gave both Dane and Nirmond another shot, to prevent a similar occurrence with them. The contents of two such pellets, he knew, would keep any human being torpid for at least four hours.

Cord withdrew his mind hastily from the direction it was turning into; but it wouldn't stay withdrawn. The thought kept coming up again, until at last he had to recognize it.

Five shots would leave the three of them completely unconscious whatever else might happen to them, until they either died from other causes or were given a counteracting agent.

Shocked, he told himself he couldn't do it. It was exactly like killing them.

But then, quite steadily, he found himself raising the gun once more, to bring the total charge for each of the three Team people up to five.

Barely thirty minutes later, he watched a raft as big as the one he rode go sliding into the foaming white waters of the Straits a few hundred yards ahead, and dart off abruptly at an angle, caught by one of the swirling currents. It pitched and spun, made some headway, and was swept aside again. And then it righted itself once more. Not like some blindly animated vegetable, Cord thought, but like a creature that struggled with intelligent purpose to maintain its chosen direction.

At least, they seemed practically unsinkable . . .

Knife in hand, he flattened himself against the platform as the Straits roared just ahead. When the platform jolted and tilted up beneath him, he rammed the knife all the way into it and hung on. Cold water rushed suddenly over him, and Grandpa shuddered like a labouring engine. In the middle of it all, Cord had the horrified notion that the raft might release its unconscious human prisoners in its struggle with the Straits. But he underestimated Grandpa in that. Grandpa also hung on.

Abruptly, it was over. They were riding a long swell, and there were three other rafts not far away. The Straits had swept them together, but they seemed to have no interest in one another's company. As Cord stood up shakily and began to strip off his clothes, they were visibly drawing apart again. The platform of one of them was half-submerged; it must have lost too much of the air that held it afloat and, like a small ship, it was foundering.

From this point, it was only a two-mile swim to the shore north of the Straits, and another mile inland from there to the Straits Head Station. He didn't know about the current; but the distance didn't seem too much, and he couldn't bring himself to leave knife and gun behind. The bay creatures loved warmth and mud, they didn't venture beyond the Straits. But Zlanti Deep bred its own killers, though they weren't often observed so close to shore.

Things were beginning to look rather hopeful.

Thin, crying voices drifted overhead, like the voices of curious cats, as Cord knotted his clothes into a tight bundle, shoes inside. He looked up. There were four of them circling there; magnified sea-going swamp bugs, each carrying an unseen rider. Probably harmless scavengers — but the ten-foot wingspread was impressive. Uneasily, Cord remembered the venomously carnivorous rider he'd left lying beside the station.

One of them dipped lazily and came sliding down towards him. It soared overhead and came back, to hover about the raft's cone.

The bug rider that directed the mindless flier hadn't been interested in him at all! Grandpa was baiting it!

Cord stared in fascination. The top of the cone was alive now with a softly wriggling mass of the scarlet, wormlike extrusions that had started sprouting before the raft left the bay. Presumably, they looked enticingly edible to the bug rider.

The flier settled with an airy fluttering and touched the cone. Like a trap springing shut, the green vines flashed up and around it, crumpling the brittle wings, almost vanishing into the long, soft body!

Barely a second later, Grandpa made another catch, this one from the sea itself. Cord had a fleeting glimpse of something like a small, rubbery seal that flung itself out of the water upon the edge of the raft, with a suggestion of desperate haste — and was flipped on instantly against the cone where the vines clamped it down beside the flier's body.

It wasn't the enormous ease with which the unexpected kill was accomplished that left Cord standing there, completely shocked. It was the shattering of his hopes to swim ashore from here. Fifty yards away, the creature from which the rubbery thing had been fleeing showed briefly on the surface, as it turned away from the raft; and that glance was all he needed. The ivory-white body and gaping jaws were similar enough to those of the sharks of Earth to indicate the pursuer's nature. The important difference was that wherever the White Hunters of the Zlanti Deep went, they went by the thousands.

Stunned by that incredible piece of bad luck, still clutching his bundled clothes, Cord stared towards shore. Knowing what to look for, he could spot the tell-tale rollings of the surface now — the long, ivory gleams that flashed through the swells and vanished again. Shoals of smaller things burst into the air in sprays of glittering desperation, and fell back.

He would have been snapped up like a drowning fly before he'd covered a twentieth of that distance!

Grandpa was beginning to eat.

Each of the dark slits down the sides of the cone was a mouth. So far only one of them was in operating condition, and the raft wasn't able to open that one very wide as yet. The first morsel had been fed into it, however: the bug rider the vines had plucked out of the flier's downy neck fur. It took Grandpa several minutes to work it out of sight, small as it was. But it was a start.

Cord didn't feel quite sane any more. He sat there, clutching his bundle of clothes and only vaguely aware of the fact that he

88

was shivering steadily under the cold spray that touched him now and then, while he followed Grandpa's activities attentively. He decided it would be at least some hours before one of that black set of mouths grew flexible and vigorous enough to dispose of a human being. Under the circumstances, it couldn't make much difference to the other human beings here; but the moment Grandpa reached for the first of them would also be the moment he finally blew the raft to pieces. The White Hunters were cleaner eaters, at any rate; and that was about the extent to which he could still control what was going to happen.

Meanwhile, there was the very faint chance that the weather station's helicopter might spot them.

Meanwhile also, in a weary and horrified fascination, he kept debating the mystery of what could have produced such a nightmarish change in the rafts. He could guess where they were going by now; there were scattered strings of them stretching back to the Straits or roughly parallel to their own course, and the direction was that of the plankton-swarming pool of the Zlanti Basin, a thousand miles to the north. Given time, even mobile lily pads like the rafts had been could make that trip for the benefit of their seedlings. But nothing in their structure explained the sudden change into alert and capable carnivores.

He watched the rubbery little seal-thing being hauled up to a mouth. The vines broke its neck; and the mouth took it in up to the shoulders and then went on working patiently at what was still a trifle too large a bite. Meanwhile, there were more thin cat-cries overhead; and a few minutes later, two more sea-bugs were trapped almost simultaneously and added to the larder. Grandpa dropped the dead sea-thing and fed himself another bug rider. The second rider left its mount with a sudden hop, sank its teeth viciously into one of the vines that caught it again, and was promptly battered to death against the platform.

Cord felt a resurge of unreasoning hatred against Grandpa. Killing a bug was about equal to cutting a branch from a tree; they had almost no life-awareness. But the rider had aroused his

89

partisanship because of its appearance of intelligent action — and it was in fact closer to the human scale in that feature than to the monstrous life form that had, mechanically, but quite successfully, trapped both it and the human beings. Then his thoughts drifted again; and he found himself speculating vaguely on the curious symbiosis in which the nerve systems of two creatures as dissimilar as the bugs and their riders could be linked so closely that they functioned as one organism.

Suddenly an expression of vast and stunned surprise appeared on his face.

Why — now he *knew!*

*   *   *

Cord stood up hurriedly, shaking with excitement, the whole plan complete in his mind. And a dozen long vines snaked instantly in the direction of his sudden motion and groped for him, taut and stretching. They couldn't reach him, but their savagely alert reaction froze Cord briefly where he was. The platform was shuddering under his feet, as if in irritation at his inaccessibility; but it couldn't be tilted up suddenly here to throw him within the grasp of the vines, as it could around the edges.

Still, it was a warning! Cord sidled gingerly around the cone till he had gained the position he wanted, which was on the forward half of the raft. And then he waited. Waited long minutes, quite motionless, until his heart stopped pounding and the irregular angry shivering of the surface of the raft-thing died away, and the last vine tendril had stopped its blind groping. It might help a lot if, for a second or two after he next started moving, Grandpa wasn't too aware of his exact whereabouts!

He looked back once to check how far they had gone by now beyond the Straits Head Station. It couldn't, he decided, be even an hour behind them. Which was close enough, by the most pessimistic count — if everything else worked out all right! He didn't try to think out in detail what that 'everything else' could include, because there were factors that simply couldn't be calculated in advance. And he had an uneasy feeling that speculating too vividly about them might make him almost incapable of carrying out his plan.

At last, moving carefully, Cord took the knife in his left hand but left the gun holstered. He raised the tightly knotted bundle of clothes slowly over his head, balanced in his right hand. With a long, smooth motion he tossed the bundle back across the cone, almost to the opposite edge of the platform.

It hit with a soggy thump. Almost immediately, the whole far edge of the raft buckled and flapped up to toss the strange object to the reaching vines.

Simultaneously, Cord was racing forward. For a moment, his attempt to divert Grandpa's attention seemed completely successful — then he was pitched to his knees as the platform came up.

He was within eight feet of the edge. As it slapped down again, he threw himself desperately forward.

An instant later, he was knifing down through cold, clear water, just ahead of the raft, then twisting and coming up again.

The raft was passing over him. Clouds of tiny sea creatures scattered through its dark jungle of feeding roots. Cord jerked back from a broad, wavering streak of glassy greenness, which was a stinger, and felt a burning jolt on his side, which meant he'd been touched lightly by another. He bumped on blindly through the slimy black tangles of hair roots that covered the bottom of the raft; then green half-light passed over him, and he burst up into the central bubble under the cone.

Half-light and foul, hot air. Water slapped around him, dragging him away again — nothing to hang on to here! Then above him, to his right, moulded against the interior curve of the cone as if it had grown there from the start, the froglike, man-sized shape of the Yellowhead.

The raft rider!

Cord reached up, caught Grandpa's symbiotic partner and guide by a flabby hind-leg, pulled himself half out of the water and struck twice with the knife, fast, while the pale-green eyes were still opening.

He'd thought the Yellowhead might need a second or so to detach itself from its host, as the bug riders usually did, before it tried to defend itself. This one merely turned its head; the mouth slashed down and clamped on Cord's left arm above the elbow. His right hand sank the knife through one staring eye, and the Yellowhead jerked away, pulling the knife from his grasp.

Sliding down, he wrapped both hands around the slimy leg and hauled with all his weight. For a moment more, the Yellowhead hung on. Then the countless neural extensions that connected it now with the raft came free in a succession of sucking, tearing sounds; and Cord and the Yellowhead splashed into the water together.

Black tangle of roots again — and two more electric burns suddenly across his back and legs! Strangling, Cord let go. Below him, for a moment, a body was turning over and over with oddly human motions; then a solid wall of water thrust him up and aside, as something big and white struck the turning body and went on.

Cord broke the surface twelve feet behind the raft. And that would have been that, if Grandpa hadn't already been slowing down.

After two tries, he floundered back up on the platform and lay there gasping and coughing awhile. There were no indications that his presence was resented now. A few lax vine-tips twitched uneasily, as if trying to remember previous functions, when he came limping up presently to make sure his three companions were still breathing; but Cord never noticed that.

They were still breathing; and he knew better than to waste time trying to help them himself. He took Grayan's heat-gun from its holster. Grandpa had come to a full stop.

Cord hadn't had time to become completely sane again, or he might have worried now whether Grandpa, violently sundered from his controlling partner, was still capable of motion on his own. Instead, he determined the approximate direction of the

Straits Head Station, selected a corresponding spot on the platform and gave Grandpa a light tap of heat.

Nothing happened immediately. Cord sighed patiently and stepped up the heat a little.

Grandpa shuddered gently. Cord stood up.

Slowly and hesitatingly at first, then with steadfast — though now again brainless — purpose, Grandpa began paddling back towards the Straits Head Station.

Glossary & Notes

The following word explanations and notes have been added to help the foreign student to gain a better understanding of the text. Each word is explained within its individual context. The number before each word is the line number on the page where the word occurs. Abbreviations: sl = slang, coll. = colloquial, adv. = adverb, adj. = adjective.

SOLE SOLUTION

Page 1

1   **brooded:** the tone of the story is set. To brood is to consider problems gloomily. Together with the title — Sole Solution reminds one of the Nazis' 'final solution' of the Jewish problem — this gives us expectations of dark, possibly horrific problems. The catalogue of problems facing the 'hero' that follows is thus prepared for.

13   **sable adj.:** a kind of furry darkness. It is often used poetically.

19   **self:** the world the hero explores is himself and the nothingness around. There is space but he is the only matter in it.

25   **ultimate scientist:** clearly the hero is either mad or is a myth. The language of this story ('eternal', 'unbearable' 'punishment' 'sin' etc.) is either the language of sickness and delusions or the language of religious myth.

Page 2

4   **strait-jacket:** one cannot move in a strait-jacket: one can only move ideas in the imagination. Strait-jackets prevent the dangerously ill from harming other people: it is a kind of

prison. Deliberate dreaming prevents the imagination from tackling real problems: it is a kind of prison too, a self-imposed prison.

11 **the problem:** how can he move when there is nowhere to go?

21 **aeons:** this word belongs to the world of religious myth, to the world of epics, to the world of gods and creations.

32 **variegated adj.:** this is a vision of a God becoming the Universe. Out of consciousness in darkness comes the variegated, many shaped, many coloured forms of the material world. This vision, this plan is the sole solution.

Page 3

5 **conflict:** this is a vision of life, of evolution as a game designed by a God in which the forces of order (the good) do battle with the forces of disorder (the bad). In that game what is 'order', the rules of the game, is decided in advance. In that game what is evolution, the sequence of events, is a battle, a tournament, a conflict. Evil is built into the system. And the system is intended to entertain ('provide experience . . . love' etc.).

7 **entities:** the parts of the body of the god figure become individual beings.

11 **experiment:** the 'game' of evolution is seen as a scientific experiment. The dream (the idea) must become physically real. The god will 'test' the dream to see if it is physically real and does provide 'warmth . . . the sound of voices'. (Compare the nuclear scientist testing whether mathematical predictions turn up in the reality he is experimenting on.)

14 **and there was light:** this is a 'play' on the Genesis creation myth. It also brings to mind a famous piece of English poetry: 'God said let Newton be and there was light!' The poetry carries the messages that understanding preceded light, or that light is a consequence of understanding, or that understanding is light, or some complex of these possibilities. Like all major messages it is highly ambiguous

if it is looked at analytically.

This science fiction story tackles the issues of an epic with the scale of a lyric poem. It deals with poetic myth and follows the usual conventions of a primitive narrative in the way its plot develops. It has five stages:

1. Orientation: lines 1-19   The problem situation.
2. Complication: lines 20-24   The hero looks on the problem and decides on his mission.
3. Evaluation: lines 24-40   The hero battles with the problem.
4. Resolution: lines 41-48   The hero's accomplishment
5. Coda: line 49   The hero's reward.

Here then is a complex work of art, a poem in prose form, well worth study. It is a far cry from the idea many people have that science fiction is comics without pictures.

WHO CAN REPLACE A MAN?

Page 4

1 **filtered into:** light and water are often described by similar words. Water filters through soil into underground rivers. Light filters through thick cloud. Filtering is a process that implies resistance.

3 **field-minder:** this is a job-name. Notice how in the second paragraph the first machine 'character' is introduced. It works by itself. It checks to see how well the work has been done. It has its own thoughts but it remains obedient.

17 **should:** notice the difference between a. what has been planned and therefore *should* happen and b. what is actually happening. It is here the crisis starts and the story begins.

22 **idly adv.:** it is bad economics for machines to be idle. Generally, *'idle'* has negative associations. We tend to use *idle* to mean 'resting when working should be going on'. *Idly* is used here to further the sense of crisis.

Page 5

3 **therefore:** notice the mechanical, logical language. It is not the language that people use. It is the language of objects about objects.

12 **chutes etc:** notice how each job has a specific type of machine to carry it out. The seed-distributor has 'grabs' to take the grain, 'scales' to measure it, and 'chutes' to deliver it.

20 **random:** 'random motion' is how we describe particles in a gas when the gas is heated, etc. It implies no sense of purpose, no sense of direction. Machines are designed for a purpose. Their actions are directed. Machines in random motion are 'sick' machines. The crisis develops.

26 **non-differentiated types:** the clerical machines are all the same. They do the same work and so they look the same. They are white-collar 'slave' machines.

29 **hatpins:** the image of the *onlooker* as a cushion full of pins is grotesque and presumably the author wants us to find it amusing. Many writers and film-makers use humour to help them build up suspense.

Page 6

4 **sliding:** another amusing image of a machine.

11 **distinction:** the machines clearly have a caste system. A machine has a set of instructions for doing a job. A machine is therefore no bigger than its job. A machine cannot grow. It can check what it understands. It understands the programme, the script it has been given. It cannot make its own script. If it is a Class Six brain it will stay a Class Six brain. It cannot become a Class Three brain.

22 **broken down:** the orders come from men. No orders means no men working to produce orders. If men are not working they must have broken down. The machine sees men as *only* existing to produce orders as field-minders only exist to mind fields.

29 **replace a man?:** this is the crisis.

34 **speculatively:** the two Class Three brains, the field-minder and the penner, are now trying to understand the crisis in terms of action. They are thus like heroes in a romance. The machines have a mission.

Page 7

5 **skittered:** this describes the way the penner moves. Each of its ten arms is involved in an up-down motion. Skitter describes the complicated result.

9 **aimlessly adv.:** the Class Six brain is clearly a machine slave. It exists only for its job. The Class Three 'heroes' have some degree of free-will. They make their own purposes, agree on them and devise a plan.

14 **lower class brains:** 'Who knows what' is a major political issue. People in power always decide what the general public

98

should know. The more they conceal information, the more authoritarian their society becomes. The penner is clearly in favour of an authoritarian 'machine-state'.

25 **without restraint:** this general picture of machines going berserk is a good instance of the black humour that can be found in many science fiction tales.

35 **all men are dead:** the comic point of this is — why should the penner believe the operator in the city? To a Class Three brain a city radio operator is God. To a Class Three brain the word 'all' and the argument 'all X is Y', are used without understanding that these generalizations have to be backed up with evidence. The penner is not looking for evidence now: it is accepting the argument.

Page 8

2 **All men were alive:** but the second hero starts a debate.

25 **little is impossible:** the Class Two Brain is to become the hero. The immediate mission is to free 'it'.

Page 9

4 **instructions:** notice how the Class Five brain is obeying the Class Three brains who are obeying the Class Two brain.

35 **destroyed:** notice the authoritarian 'character' of the penner is being developed. The assenting of the other machines follows. The Class Two brain now has its army under the command of the penner.

Page 10

15 **fissionable blasting materials:** nuclear explosives.

16 **use them:** the Operator is happy to use a little nuclear action.

18 **behind it:** the speed of the lorry is breaking the sound barrier. Its message is thus interrupted by the explosions of the sound barrier being broken.

25 **statement:** the penner is enjoying its power.

Page 11

6   **field-minder:** the field minder is more impulsive than the penner. The mission of the heroes has been complicated. The penner wants to alter course: the field-minder to go on. Note the field minder believes they can destroy a Class One Brain.

Page 12

6   **penner:** notice it is the penner who takes the decision.

13   **dust:** notice in this paragraph what the presupposition of the story is: what technology has done to the earth.
     Many science fiction stories are the dramatized implications of some effect that technology has produced.

24   **mountains:** mountains are climbed in the pursuit of truth in many myths.

Page 13

4   **information:** machines exist in order to process information. The flier's information is a major twist in the plot and the first truth they encounter on the mountain.

18   **slower adv.:** those who have read Pilgrim's Progress may see a grotesque similarity between the machines and the pilgrims.

34   **no further use:** the penner — perhaps the villain of the story — meets his just deserts. The 'moral' is: machines should learn to repair themselves. The servicer should be built in.

Page 14

34   **immediately!:** the ending is ironical in two ways. If the penner had not broken down would the machines have obeyed? In having the penner killed off, the author neatly dodges this issue.

THE FORGOTTEN ENEMY

Page 15

1   **thudded:** writers often begin action stories with vigorous physical verbs. Notice the sequence 'thudded ... freezing ... rasping ... crashing' in the first paragraph. It is as if the writer was trying to imitate the loud beating of the heart, to shock the reader into a state of awareness.

6   **he listened intently:** the problem situation is developed. The hero listens for the sound: but it does not repeat itself and reveal where it comes from. Did the hero imagine it? How can he find out?

16   **guarded:** why should he have to *guard* the volumes? Who is he protecting them from? What are they?

23   **wantonness:** wanton implies extravagance and is often used to describe prostitutes together with the word 'brazen'. The wantonness of thunder is the obviousness, the way in which the sound is repeated, redisplayed and comes from many sources.

Page 16

7   **quench:** the hero's reading of the problem is revealed. He has been alone guarding his books for twenty years waiting for men to return to a place where the ice had driven other people away. He has not seen himself as lost: he has seen himself as waiting in hope. But he also has thoughts that would put out, quench, the flame of his hope.

11   **Battersea Power Station:** this is known for its large gasometers by the banks of the Thames, in West London. The image here is of London in the grip of an ice age. The stacks (chimneys) of the power station are among the highest points in London: the professor has a 'high' degree of understanding of what has happened to London; that is why the stacks *challenge* 'his supremacy'.

18 **churning:** this describes what happens when snow gets caught in the moving rotors of the helicopter.

20 **the North:** the North, like Dust, is capitalized. The capital letter draws attention to the importance of the concept to the hero. The North (of ice and snow) is a major fact: the Dust was a major event.

Page 17

14 **cosmic dust:** the Dust is now explained.

22 **floundering:** the act of walking uncertainly. The snow may or may not support the weight of the professor.

35 **ordeal:** the way in which problems test you is an ordeal. The ordeal referred to here is the ordeal of listening for messages.

Page 18

10 **'hiss':** the random noise you hear on a radio between radio stations, is everywhere.

19 **tenuous:** the Heaviside Layer is that part of the ionosphere from which radio waves are bounced off. The layer is not a substance though and therefore it is tenuous, hard to grasp.

Page 19

18 **revived:** brought to life again.

32 **lattice:** the bars and cross-bars of the gate.

35 **incongruous:** out of proportion. The white ferret he remembers is incongruous, because it is so much smaller than the polar bear.

Page 21

5 **poignantly:** intense, piercing, sad.

19 **ominous:** a threatening sign.

32 **rearguard action:** a rearguard action is one fought by a group of soldiers at the back of a retreating army.

Page 23

2 **... weren't Mom's words:** Mom spoke the words; Dad had the idea. Dad's idea came out of Mom's mouth.

5 **Martian pebbles:** the action begins on Mars.

9 **trembling hands:** hands tremble with emotion or with illness.

12 **stud:** notice how simple technology is. You press a button or stud: and off goes the boat.

18 **family rocket:** in this story people have rockets like we, today, have motor cars.

24 **funny:** funny in the sense of unusual.

25 **a look ...:** Dad is happy in a way his son has not seen before. The light shines in his eyes: the wrinkles are laughter-wrinkles not worry-wrinkles.

Page 24

5 **A million years:** we can travel in time as well as space. Numbers can express amount (a million = a lot of time) in general terms.

11 **Martian weatherman:** does this mean the climate, the weather, is artificially controlled?

12 **... he was pleased:** you can just look at ruins. Only the light changes. A ruined city is one that is not used by people. It is not growing or changing.

13 **futile adj.:** the dead city is futile because it is not doing, not achieving anything. The stones of the city are just stones: the dead city is sleeping on the landscape.

19 **Dad got a frightened look:** the bird is life, is motion, is unpredictable. It reminds Dad of an unexpected rocket. The bird of life = the rocket of death.

21 **Earth and the war:** perhaps this is what Dad is escaping from.

27 **tarantula:** a tarantula is a poisonous spider. A small,

bunched hand is like the six legs of a spider. But why a *poisonous* spider?

31 **vast adult mechanism:** Timothy doesn't understand what makes his father 'tick'. He doesn't understand his motives. His father's motives are like the principles that make a machine work. To a child the behaviour of his father is as strange as the behaviour of a machine or mechanism.

31 **the man:** notice how this description is a. through the eyes of the child (eyes like marbles) and b. through the eyes of the author (columnar legs = legs like columns).

Page 25

14 **war swims along etc.:** the author uses metaphors to describe the setting and the action. He also, here, puts metaphor into the mouths of his characters: Dad sees a fish feeding and thinks of war as a mouth eating up the earth.

26 **Timothy scowled:** Timothy like most children is spontaneous: the parents use 'looks' to control one another. The parents have a language of looks: Timothy does not like this language.

33 **a pulse beating time:** a nerve twitching. A sign of strong emotions being controlled.

34 **Mother:** the metaphors used to describe the mother (thoughts = fish; eyes = deep cool water; opening of blouse =shape of flower) are metaphors of nature, of peace, of growth. It is a romantic picture, a poetic portrait. Mother is not only a mother: she is Mother.

Page 26

17 **penned:** here means contained. Sheep pens are movable gates used to fence in sheep.

20 **beetles in a dry skull:** the story is a poem in prose. Like a poem it moves from the world of description (the cities) to the world of interpretation (the cities are like beetles, the dry desert and air around and beneath the cities are like skulls).

The meaning of the cities in their surroundings, in the mind of the travellers is like beetles in a skull. The memories are shaken together in the mind, as the beetles are shaken together in the skull.

23   **. . . to fish:** the irony. To travel millions of miles for something so simple as fishing! Is Mars the nearest place where man can fish? Are the rivers of earth so polluted?

24   **vacation:** how long is a vacation?

27   **veil of the vacation:** the parents have told the children they are going on a holiday. A holiday is a time for adventure but a short time for adventure. Do the parents see themselves as on holiday? Or are they looking for a new life? Notice the metaphor: explanation = veil: truth = face beneath. Is the truth, the face, a frightening truth? What is the explanation (the veil) hiding? To the two younger children explanation = truth: they do not see the veil.

Page 27

1   **his face looked etc:** Dad is almost a ruin now. What is he hearing on the radio?

10   **jounced:** an invented word: *'bounced'* and *'jumped'* are combined to make a new word with both their meanings. Bounced implies an object only and not an intention. Jumped is a conscious act. Jounced is a conscious intended bouncing.

11   **funk sl.:** a slang term for fear, a fear that prevents action.

19   **into hiding:** are they being chased? By whom? Martians?

Page 28

21   **a series of dead cities:** when a story is repeated many times it becomes a myth. Is this story a story about a journey through hell? Through death? Is it like a Greek myth?

Page 29

11   **centrifugal:** why centrifugal? All fountains are centrifugal.

105

26 **lethal:** something which kills. The revelation, the new understanding, is that civilisation on earth has ended. People may still be alive but the radio is dead because the cities that make radio stations possible are dead. The 'lethal revelation' is *not* the *fact* of the end of civilization: it is the *understanding*, the interpretation; what it means to the child.

Page 30

6 **still a game:** the game is an escape, a way of reducing the problem to something playful.

9 **be careful of your sister:** is Mom pregnant? How does Dad know the child will be a girl? Note the word 'later'. It implies, entails that the family survives beyond the present moment of narration.

16 **I'll hunt for Bert Edwards:** Dad has planned the escape with friends. Two families is a basis for society: two families — one with sons and one with daughters. This is the first positive twist in the story: you can think of a story as moving from side to side, twisting its way between negative (problems) and positive (plans) poles. 'Realistic' stories end with a negative twist with problems: 'romantic' stories end with a positive twist, with plans. Good reading is anticipating a twist: good writing is writing that does not allow us to guess too easily what is coming next and so surprises us. A novel is something new, unpredictable, and therefore entertaining.

Page 31

10 **Darn coll.:** a polite substitute (a euphemism) for damn. Here it is, perhaps, a *hopeful* substitute: Dad doesn't want to believe in a 'damned' planet. 'The whole darn X' is a kind of exasperated half-curse that people use when they want to complain about the problems of some possession or relationship.

13 **unimpeachable monarchs:** there is nobody to judge them. They *are* the law-makers.

106

23   **Engulfed them:** this describes the physical movement of the letters in the fire: frightened animals leaping and letters jumping in the fire = the letters are alive. The letters are alive in the sense that they represent descriptions of real events made by real people. It is not just the marks on paper that are burning, it is the knowledge they represent. Notice how a metaphor like this crystallises the theme of the story.

Page 32

2   **I'm burning a way of life:** notice how a metaphor (see 23) is followed by an explanation in this story. The author introduces a theme in a metaphor and develops the theme in dialogue. By having a father talking to his sons the author is able to explain, to *teach* the meaning of his metaphor. Many metaphors in science fiction are used not to describe but to explore: the basic issue they explore is 'where is Technology taking us?' Much science fiction is trying to give a value for X, in the following equation:

$$\text{Technology} + \text{War} = \text{X}$$

3   **... burned clean off earth:** notice how the explanation of a metaphor is itself metaphorical. A metaphor is one way, the major poetic way perhaps, of expressing correspondence: the correspondence here is between the little fire Dad has caused and the huge fire, the holocaust, that War has caused on earth. Dad is burning the past that burned the earth. Dad's fire is a gesture, a symbolic action. The old knowledge led to disaster: so he is burning the disaster.

30   **was gone like a warm black butterfly:** the butterfly is often used by poets as a symbol of resurrection. A butterfly is new life, a new form of life, emerging from the crysallis. *But,* this is a black butterfly, a symbol of death not resurrection. But what has died is useless. What use is a map of the earth when the earth is covered with flames? Who are Dad and his family now anyway? They are no longer Earth people. The fire symbolizes their renunciation of Earth.

Page 34

Title **Compassion Circuit:** notice the unusual juxtaposition of compassion (human feelings) and circuit (electronic pathway). This suggests a machine with feelings is to appear in the story.

11 **nitwit coll.:** person not using his wits properly. A term of mild abuse.

12 **spick and span coll.:** clean and tidy.

16 **diehard:** rigid, inflexible, obstinate. A person whose ideas die hard.

Page 35

9 **enlightenment:** notice this follows on from the word 'revelation'. (Perhaps the heroine is in hospital because she finds it hard to live in a world of machines?) 'Truth' is 'revealed'. The heroine is 'enlightened'. She understands what other people accept.

31 **what pattern?:** you can buy robots. The robots are mass-produced in different patterns. It is like buying clothes.

Page 36

1 **compassion–protection circuit:** the language of machine description. Notice how the properties, the characteristics of the machine are described: the machine has the quality of being aware of people's feelings to a high degree — hence high-sensibility (compare with high-fidelity stereo for example). The robot is the result of a job of work: hence 'high-sensibility job'. The robot is the result of recent technical progress: hence 'quite novel'. The robot will not just obey its patient: it will decide itself whether the patient should be obeyed: a patient who issued a violent order, for example, would not be obeyed: hence 'contra-balanced,

compassion-protection'. The nurse robot will decide what is best for the patient!

12   **a hole coll.:** a hole in his savings. A common metaphor (the money is taken from the savings and leaves a hole).

Page 37

4   **standard . . . patterns:** these are the memory units that are installed in the robot to carry out routines, like serving food and washing up. They are 'standard domestic' because they programme the machine to perform basic household tasks. They are 'pseudo-memory' because they are remembered but not reflected on, not thought about.

27   **wadding:** padding. Perhaps soft cotton to protect the robot from damage.

34   **sleeping beauty:** there is an English fairy story about a girl who has been asleep for a very long time. The story is called The Sleeping Beauty.

Page 38

10   **flawless:** perfect. The word 'flawless' is often used to describe precious stones, like pearls.

13   **contraption:** a machine or device. Something contrived, made up.

33   **indelicacy:** sexually rude.

Page 39

32   **foible:** strange piece of behaviour usually seen as a weakness.

Page 40

7   **euphemism:** a polite way of talking about delicate matters (sex, the lavatory etc.). Perhaps if the machine does not use euphemism it is not so highly-sensible?

13   **computing . . . shunting:** the way the computer mind of the robot works. The computer mind *is* a machine. The word 'shunting' is often used to describe how trucks on a railway

are pushed to a destination: it reinforces the machine nature of the robot's mind.

19 **not your fault:** note 'fault' implies blame: 'misfortune' implies things go wrong but it is not the fault of the person concerned.

21 **we are stronger etc.:** notice how the contrast in this passage between Janet (the weak sickly human being) and Hester (the perfectly working robot) is the central issue of the story spelled out in detail. The story has taken two extremes (not an ordinary person but a sick one: not an ordinary robot but one with a compassion circuit) to deal with the question — can machines take over from us? Are machines a higher state of evolution than men?

35 **precariously adv.:** the phrase 'a precarious hold' is often used to talk of people who do not have 'a strong grip' on themselves and who are often ill.

Page 41

28 **patient:** an ironic pun. Janet is the patient (the sick person) of Hester. Hester listens with patience and so is the 'patient Hester'. But Hester is the nurse, the one in control, an agent not a patient.

29 **heart:** Hester sees the heart as a machine for pumping blood around the body. Heart also has the meaning of feeling, emotion, courage. Hester ignores this.

Page 42

19 **impeccable:** this robot has a compassion-circuit as well. It is not only capable of expressing sympathy, it can also do it 'perfectly', impeccably. This implies a performance such as an actor gives.

Page 43

12 **success:** who decides on what is a successful operation? This is where the 'twist' in the story begins.

22 **outcome:** but what will come out?
30 **adamant:** a refusal to budge in an argument or discussion. Resistant.

Page 44
35 **compassion-circuit:** what the C.C. has is feeling without insight. C.C. is sorry but the C.C. doesn't see why.

Page 45
9 **will sign it:** the robot predicts what the human being will do. The robots are in charge.

ROBBIE

Page 46
2 **chubby adj.:** healthy but fat, often used to describe babies.
7 **clump:** grouping, close clustering of trees.
18 **clump clump:** here the word is used to describe a sound, a heavy, muffled sound. Notice the human child and the machine 'friend' as the characters the author will explore. The machine friend is given prominence by the title. Is the author suggesting we should identify with Robbie? Are we to try and see the story through the 'eyes' of the machine?

Page 47
11 **veer:** to move away from the desired direction.
22 **dishevelled:** untidy, disarranged.
24 **torso:** the body.
30 **parallelopid:** a moving four-sided object.

Page 48
6 **gingham:** cloth with pattern of checks.
16 **hurt:** is Robbie hurt or pretending to be? Is the robot playing games like a child does or like an adult does?

Page 51
23 **disconsolate:** sad. Unable to be consoled.

Page 54
5 **huff coll.:** a fit of anger mixed with justification. Mild anger.
11 **Robbie:** is Robbie becoming the hero of the story? Here is a point in the story where we can identify with him and feel sympathetic.

Page 55
3 **ensuing:** following.

7 **visivox:** vision and voice. A kind of cinema.
9 **winced:** to wince is to frown, to screw up the face, in response to something painful.

Page 57

13 **flounced:** used often to describe the angry walk of a woman.
14 **boiling mad coll.:** In a rage.
32 **pining away:** to think sadly of the past, to mourn, and to become, usually, thin and ill.

Page 58

8 **perk her up:** to bring Gloria back into happiness. To give her energy and purpose.
10 **frying pavements:** the pavements of New York are so hot they are like frying pans.
12 **pounds:** five pounds in weight.
34 **taxi - gyro:** a helicopter used as a taxi.

Page 60

2 **bout:** an attack of coughing.
15 **dissipating:** to dissipate energy is to use it to do too many jobs, for example.
29 **peremptorily:** sharply, in a commanding tone.

Page 61

4 **ogled:** to stare intensely. Often used to describe the way men look at girls they do not know but like the look of.
6 **revel:** to be happily entertained.
23 **witchery:** devices created by science that seem to be magical if you don't understand the principles behind the design.
32 **full of the maternal genes:** Gloria is like her mother.

Page 62

33 **pot-hooks coll.:** shorthand.

Page 65

3 **. . . vest buttons strained:** George is puffing out his chest.

34 **Gave vent:** produced.

Page 65

4 **sluices:** the man is being described as if he were a machine. Sluices are gates in a dam holding back water. When they are opened the water ('the flood of explanation' here) floods out. This metaphor expresses the main problem, the central uncertainty, that the story is about: What is the difference between man and machine?

22 **faltered:** to stop doing something through loss of interest or loss of skill. It is a word usually used to describe human action.

Page 67

1 **precision:** a robot is a precision-made device. It is precisely designed — there are no parts that do not function. It is precisely programmed — it is told by its memory exactly what to do and what steps are necessary to do it. It can act precisely — it has all the knowledge that its designers have slowly worked out over the years and it can use this knowledge with great speed. Notice how one man — George — takes too long to react *whereas* the robot (the result of the thinking of many men) acts instantly.

19 **engineered:** an engineer plans the creation of an object or service. He makes things come about.

23 **Robbie wasn't designed . . .:** Mrs Weston believes that robots can only be designed for specific purposes. A robot can only be designed for engineering or for domestic work: not both.

Page 68

1 **lovingly:** what is a loving robot?

Page 69

1   **A green-winged downy thing:** why begin with this flying 'thing'? Why a 'thing' not a bird?

3   **A fourteen-year-old human being:** why use the term 'human being'? What other beings will there be in the story.

9   **Bug-rider:** Why *semi*-parasitical? What does the bug rider do in addition to living off the bug? Does it control it? Use it? To what purpose? What kind of symbiosis is going on?

14 **what fascinating things etc.:** a major theme in science fiction. How the scientist explores *not* what is happening in the natural cycle of events *but* what he can cause to happen. The 'pure' scientist is looking for problems to investigate: the 'applied' scientist is looking for knowledge he can use to make something new. The applied scientist, the technologist, *controls* knowlege. The technologist produces communicating machines like television: he also produces killing machines like atom bombs. Science fiction stories can be seen as warnings to technologists: they tease out the human consequences that follow from the creation of machines that can be used to kill not only people but ideals and values. Cord is a technologist: the issue is how far-sighted will he be?

16 **hampered:** hindered, limited, prevented from achieving a purpose. What hampers Cord? What purpose is being hampered?

19 **The Station:** a place where knowledge is controlled. The team of researchers have to do 'practical' research. 'Practical' implies short-term research to solve immediate problems. It implies the questions are fixed, were fixed, are yesterday's questions. 'Practical' implies blinkers. The horse sees the 'road' ahead more clearly with blinkers. Cord does not want to wear blinkers. He does not want to travel down someone else's road.

115

24   **central lock:** Way out.

Page 70

10   **a tiny scarlet demon:** is it a demon, an evil, murderous
      creature? Or is it a creature defending its world and
      justifiably angry at the shooting down of the bug? (The bug
      rider presumably would not 'know' that the shot was an
      anaesthetic shot, not a killing shot.)

31   **you'd be sunk coll.:** in trouble.

Page 71

9   **treadcar:** car with a tread like a tank for travelling over
      rough country?

10   **bagged coll.:** captured.

11   **hurriedly flew:** Cord is intellectually free but socially
      short-sighted. He hasn't seen till now how other people see
      him. He has been wearing social blinkers.

27   **That was as far as:** the team is interested in phenomena only
      to the extent that they seem useful.

Page 72

3   **Grandpa:** What is Grandpa? What is a plant animal? Is
      Grandpa a monster *only* in the sense of size (monster =
      huge)? Why is the story called Grandpa? Is Grandpa to be
      the hero? The villain? Notice the underlying issue: how *far*
      should man 'use' other forms of life?

4   **hiding:** is Grandpa hiding? Or has Cord hidden him?

10   **The rafts tend:** Nirmond sees Grandpa as a feeding system,
      not as a conscious being or a feeling being.

15   **lurched:** implies a sudden, crude, clumsy action.

19   **unauthorised tours:** notice what Grandpa meant to Cord. To
      Cord, Grandpa was a sailing vessel, a means of exploring.

26   **beasties:** a diminuitive of beasts. Diminuitives are usually
      used to express familiarity with someone or something.

28   **snapper:** presumably an aggressive sea creature with a

mouth or claw that snaps at other forms of life that disturb it
or that might provide food.

Page 74

2   **Earth etc.:** notice how capital letters are used to give ideas
the force of laws.

13 **they didn't usually move:** the 'complication' stage of the story
begins here. Something surprising, unforseen, has happened.
Grandpa is not behaving in the way Nirmond expects
(compare with note on page 71 line 10). Perhaps (see note
on page 69 line 1) Grandpa has a rider, like the flying thing
that opens the story?

31 **goaded:** a goad is, for example, a sharp pointed stick for
driving cattle. A goad is a means of using pain to control the
movement of an animal.

33 **He's sprouting:** surprise is often a result of change. Change is
sometimes a product of chance — we can't predict this kind
of change very easily. Chance is sometimes a result of a
natural cycle —chrysalis into butterfly, for example, — and
this can be predicted through study. Change is sometimes a
result of a plan — work produces changes in the state of
matter so that a mineral becomes a gold ring. The issue here
is which kind of change has taken place. 'Sprouting' suggests
natural plant-like change.

Page 74

1   **saurian adj.:** lizard-like.

3   **kinky:** twisted like a corkscrew.

7   **Grandpa looked unhealthy:** perhaps the change is the result
of illness? Perhaps the illness is the result of the goads that
Cord used to drive Grandpa?

13 **his hackles were still up:** animal metaphor. To raise your
hackles is to show anger or fear (some animals swell up to
frighten their foes).

20 **quibbling:** arguing over a small point.

117

Page 75

26 **nettle-streamers:** nettles — plants that sting.

Page 76

7 **brackish:** slightly salt.

18 **mutated grains:** changed by man, in this instance.

24 **a flare:** upsurge.

Page 78

1 **sissy sl.:** afraid, like a girl.

9 **carapaced:** like a tortoises's shell.

23 **pennants:** flags of identification.

Page 79

25 **The key:** the answer to the planet's biology.

Page 87

4 **swell:** wave.

10 **foundering:** beginning to sink.

31 **extrusions:** forced out substances.

Page 92

10 **neural:** of the nerves.

18 **something big and white:** one of the shark-like white hunters of the Zlanti Deep.

25 **lax:** inattentive. Grandpa has returned to his vegetable state — without mind or purpose.

Page 93

4 **stepped up:** increased.